HANDBOOK OF VARIABLES FOR ENVIRONMENTAL IMPACT ASSESSMENT

HANDBOOK OF VARIABLES FOR ENVIRONMENTAL IMPACT ASSESSMENT

by

LARRY W. CANTER

Director & Professor
School of Civil Engineering and
  Environmental Science
University of Oklahoma
Norman, Oklahoma

LOREN G. HILL

Director and Professor
University of Oklahoma Biological Station
University of Oklahoma
Norman, Oklahoma

ANN ARBOR SCIENCE
PUBLISHERS INC
P.O. BOX 1425 • ANN ARBOR, MICH. 48106

PREFACE

The objective of this Handbook is to provide (1) a comprehensive listing of variables relevant to the environmental quality objective of water resource planning; and (2) descriptions of measurement, prediction and assessment techniques for the selected variables when used for environmental impact assessments of water and related land-management studies.

Variables, or assessment variables, refer to those characteristics of the environment used to describe the baseline environmental setting and upon which impacts may occur. This Handbook is organized by section into those variables associated with the terrestrial, aquatic, air and human interface environments. For each of the 62 selected variables, information is presented on their definition, measurement needs for establishing baseline conditions, and impact prediction and assessment. Functional curves are also included for most of the variables. A functional curve represents an empirical relationship between objective measurements of a variable and a subjective evaluation of the quality (good to bad) of that variable in the environmental setting.

This Handbook is intended for use by professionals working on environmental impact studies. Even though the orientation is to water resources, the Handbook is of general value due to the broad applicability and importance of the 62 variables selected. The Handbook could also be used in upper division or graduate level University courses dealing with environmental impact assessments/statements.

Larry W. Canter

Loren G. Hill

ACKNOWLEDGMENTS

This Handbook is a summary of work performed under Purchase Order No. DACW39-77-M-1631 titled "Variables for Environmental Quality Account," dated February, 1977, between the U.S. Army Engineer Waterways Experiment Station (WES) and the authors. The research was sponsored by the Office, Chief of Engineers, U.S. Army, Washington, DC, and directed by the Environmental Laboratory, WES

The authors express their gratitude to the University of Oklahoma for its support during the preparation of this Handbook. Special acknowledgement is given to Mr. Charles Solomon, Mr. Billy Colbert, and Ms. Sue Richardson, WES, for their professional advice throughout this study. In addition, the authors acknowledge Mrs. Edna Rothschild, Mrs. Madelon Carmack, Ms. Kristi Smith and Ms. Susan Wilkerson for their typing assistance in the preparation of this manuscript. Special thanks are extended to Mrs. Jerry Lawrence for her efforts in the preparation of the author and subject indexes. Finally the authors thank their families for their encouragement in the process of developing this Handbook.

LARRY W. CANTER, P.E., is Director and Professor, School of Civil Engineering and Environmental Science, University of Oklahoma, Norman. Dr. Canter received his PhD in Environmental Health Engineering from the University of Texas, MS in Sanitary Engineering from the University of Illinois, and BE in Civil Engineering from Vanderbilt University. Before joining the faculty of the University of Oklahoma in 1969, he was on the faculty of Tulane University and was a sanitary engineer in the U.S. Public Health Service.

Dr. Canter has published several books, including *Water Resources Assessment--Methodology & Technology Sourcebook* (Ann Arbor Science Publishers, Inc., 1979), and is the author of numerous papers, research reports and chapters.

His research includes environmental impact assessment, groundwater pollution control, and solid hazardous waste management. Dr. Canter has been project director or co-director of some 20 externally sponsored research projects at the University of Oklahoma, and conducts courses on environmental impact assessment.

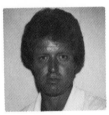

LOREN G. HILL is Director of the University of Oklahoma Biological Station, Professor of Zoology, and Curator of Fishes at the University of Oklahoma. He obtained his BS degree from West Texas State University in 1961, his MS degree from the University of Arkansas in 1963, and his PhD degree from the University of Louisville in 1966. Specializing in Ichthyology and Aquatic Ecology, Dr. Hill has published more than 50 papers in scientific journals on many aspects of fishery ecology, and was Editor for the Annals of the Oklahoma Academy of Science. He has served as President of the Organization of Inland Biological Field Stations (1970-1972) and also as President of the Southwestern Association of Naturalists (1976-1978).

Dr. Hill has worked extensively in the area of environmental assessment and as consultant to private environmental assessment firms, the U.S. Army Corps of Engineers, Civil Service Commission, Department of Army, and the Environmental Protection Agency. In 1979, he was named the first recipient of the Regents Award for Superior Professional Achievement and University Service.

To Donna, Doug, Steve, and Greg

To Kenyon   and Kelton

CONTENTS

INTRODUCTION

The environmental impact assessment process involves five activities. The first is an understanding of the legal bases and procedural requirements for the process. Second is a description of the environmental setting where the proposed action is to take place. Assessment variables, or more simply, variables, refer to those characteristics of the environment used to describe the baseline environmental setting and upon which impacts may occur. The third activity in the process, and the one which requires the greatest scientific application of technology, is impact prediction and assessment. The impacts of each of the alternatives being evaluated on each of the variables should be predicted and interpreted. The fourth activity involves the aggregation of impact information on each alternative. Based on this aggregated information as well as technical and economic considerations, the alternative to become the proposed action is selected. The final activity involves the preparation of an environmental impact assessment report (EIA) describing the procedure and findings. The report could also be an environmental impact statement (EIS) is no EIA is required; if an EIA is prepared, information from it could be used in the EIS (Canter, 1977).

Appropriate selection and use of variables is an important component of the environmental impact assessment process. Variables represent key features of the activities involving description of the environmental setting, impact prediction and assessment, and selection of the proposed action. To provide a structure to the variables considered, the environment can be compartmentalized into physical-chemical, biological, esthetic, and socio-economic features. For example, for water resources projects the variables can be grouped into the Environmental Quality (EQ), Social Well-Being (SWB), and Regional Development (RD) accounts. The EQ account primarily addresses the natural environment and includes physical-chemical, biological and esthetic variables; the SWB and RD accounts are oriented to the man-made environment and include socio-economic variables.

The objective of this Handbook is to present a comprehensive list of variables for addressing the physical-chemical, biological, and esthetic features of the environment. The variables are organized according to the EQ account for water resources projects, however, their use can be for any type of project. Use of the variables in this Handbook will enable a systematic

1

consideration and evaluation of the environmental consequences of project development and operation.

To provide a structuce for considering and selecting the variables presented in this Handbook, four categories were chosen, namely, terrestrial, aquatic, air, and human interface. The terrestrial and aquatic categories include physical-chemical and biological variables; the air category includes physical-chemical variables; and the human interface category includes esthetic variables along with noise and historical and archeo-logical resources. These categories of the environment were used in a water resources environmental impact assessment methodology (Solomon, et al., 1977). Each variable included is grouped into either the terrestrial, aquatic, air or human interface categories; and described in terms of measurement, prediction and evaluation considerations.

To select variables for inclusion in this Handbook, a master list of 189 potential ones shown in Table 1 was assembled The list was compiled following review of several environmental impact assessment methodologies. One methodology which included each listed variable is shown in Table 1; in many cases indivi-dual variables were listed in each of several methodologies. Final selection of the variables for inclusion in this Handbook was made following consideration of the general importance of the variables, the impacts of water projects, and the information needed to accomplish impact prediction and assessment. The selected variables are shown in Table 1 by an asterisk. Table 2 summarizes the totals for the considered and presented variables. Figure 1 displays the hierarchical structure of the selected variables.

For each of the 62 selected variables in this Handbook, information is presented on their definition, measurement needs for establishing baseline conditions, and impact prediction and **assessment**. Functional curves are also included for most of the variables. A functional curve represents an empirical relationship between objective measurements of a variable and a subjective evaluation of the quality (good to bad) of that variable in the environmental setting. Objective measurements are plotted on the x-axis, while the subjective quality index is presented on the y-axis. The quality index is presented on a a scale from 0.0 to 1.0 with 0.0 representing low or undesirable quality and 1.0 representing high or desirable quality. Usage of functional curves in environmental impact studies provides an approach for systematically describing the quality of the existing environment as well as assessing the potential impacts of projects. The functional curves which are present-ed are considered to be generally applicable. Individual functional curves may need to be modified to address specific environmental conditions in a given region or locale, and professional judgement would be required to accomplish necessary modifications.

This Handbook primarily serves as a source document for information on pertinent variables for environmental impact assessment studies. It is organized by section into those variables associated with the terrestrial, aquatic, air, and human interface environments. Selected references on background information for each of the 62 variables are also identified and contained in the last section. Usage of the information contained herein requires professional judgement in application.

TABLE 1:   LIST OF VARIABLES CONSIDERED FOR
ENVIRONMENTAL QUALITY ACCOUNT
(* = selected variables)

TERRESTRIAL

I.   Populations

   *1.   Crops (Battelle EES)
    2.   Vegetation (Battelle Dredging Impact Assessment Method)
    3.   Trees (Lower Mississippi Valley Division - LMVD)
    4.   Shrubs (Bureau of Reclamation)
    5.   Grasses (LMVD)
    6.   Forbs (Bureau of Reclamation)
    7.   Ground cover (LMVD)
   *8.   **Natural vegetation** (Battelle EES)
    9.   Animal life (Bureau of Reclamation)
   10.   Browsers and grazers (Battelle EES)
   11.   Big game (Bureau of Reclamation)
   12.   Upland game (Bureau of Reclamation)
   13.   Fur-bearing animals (Bureau of Reclamation)
   14.   Game mammals (Battelle Dredging Impact Assessment
         Method)
  *15.   Herbivorous mammals (Battelle EES)
  *16.   Carnivorous mammals (Battelle EES)
  *17.   Upland game birds (Battelle EES)
  *18.   Predatory birds (U.S. Army - CERL)

II.   Habitats/Land Use

    1.   Terrestrial habitat (Battelle Water Resources Project)
    2.   Wildlife habitat (Soil Conservation Service - SCS)
    3.   Bottomland forest (LMVD)---composite indicator based
         on following 11 factors:

                Species Associations
                Percent Mast-Bearing Trees
                Percent Coverage of Understory
                Diversity of Understory
                Percent coverage by Groundcover
                Diversity of Groundcover
                Number of Trees $\geqslant$18 in. dbh/ac
                Percent of Trees $\geqslant$18 in. dbh

Frequency of Inundation
Quantity of Edge
Mean Distance to Edge

*4. Upland forest (LMVD)---composite indicator based on following 10 factors:

Species Association
Percent Mast-Bearing Trees
Percent Coverage of Understory
Diversity of Understory
Percent Coverage of Groundcover
Diversity of Groundcover
Number of Trees ≥16 in. dbh/ac
Percent of Trees ≥16 in. dbh
Quantity of Edge
Mean Distance to Edge

*5. Open (non-forest) lands (LMVD)---composite indicator based on the following four factors:

Land Use
Diversity of Land Use
Quantity of Edge
Mean Distance to Edge

6. Land/water interface (Battelle Water Resources Project)
7. Drawdown zone (Battelle Water Resources Project)
8. Land use (Battelle EES)
9. Woodland (SCS)
10. Cropland (SCS)
11. Pastureland (SCS)
12. Rangeland (SCS)
13. Wildlife land (SCS)
14. Urban land (SCS)
15. Recreation land (SCS)
16. Other land uses; e.g., surface mined land (SCS)
17. Water (SCS)

III. Land Quality/Soil Erosion

1. Topography (Battelle EES)
2. Flood hazard/flood plains (SCS)
3. Deposition (SCS)
4. Subsidence (Battelle Dredging Impact Assessment Method)
5. Toxic materials (Battelle Dredging Impact Assessment Method)
*6. Soil erosion (Battelle EES)

    7. Soil texture/permeability (Housing and Urban Development - HUD)
    8. Soil nutrients - NO_3 and PO_4 (SCS)
*9. Soil chemistry - nutrients, salinity, SO_4, alkalinity, Fe, Mn and B (SCS)
  10. Quality for specific uses; e.g., cropland, pastureland, rangeland, woodland, wildlife land, urban, recreation, other (SCS)
  11. Wetlands (SCS)
  12. Geological resources (Bureau of Reclamation)
*13. Mineral extraction (SCS)
  14. Unique geological features (HUD)
  15. Depth to impermeable layers (HUD)
  16. Special land features - sanitary landfill, coastal zones/shorelines, mine dumps/spoil areas, and prime agricultural land (HUD)
  17. Natural hazard (CERL)

IV. Critical Community Relationships

    1. Food web index (Battelle EES)
*2. Species diversity (Battelle EES)
    3. Ecosystem productivity (Tulsa District)
    4. Ecosystem diversity and stability (Tulsa District)
    5. Nutrient cycling (HUD)

V. Threatened and/or Endangered Species

    1. Threatened and/or endangered species (Battelle EES)

VI. Pests

    1. Pest species (Battelle EES)

AQUATIC

I. Populations

*1. Natural vegetation (Battelle EES)
*2. Wetland vegetation (Battelle Dredging Impact Assessment Method)
*3. Zooplankton (Battelle Dredging Impact Assessment Method)
*4. Phytoplankton (Battelle Dredging Impact Assessment Method)
    5. Algae (Environmental Impact Center)
    6. Fish (Battelle Dredging Impact Assessment Method)
*7. Sport fish (LMVD and Battelle EES)
*8. Commercial fisheries (Battelle EES)

*9. Intertidal organisms (Battelle Dredging Impact
Assessment Method)
*10. Benthos/epibenthos (Battelle Dredging Assessment
Method)
*11. Waterfowl (Battelle EES)

II. Habitats

1. Lotic - flowing (Tulsa District)
2. Lentic - standing (Tulsa District)
3. Change from lotic to lentic (Battelle Water Resources
Project)
4. River characteristics (Battelle EES)
*5. Stream (LMVD)---composite indicator based on following
8 factors:

Sinuosity
Dominant Centrarchid
Mean Low Water Width
Turbidity
TDS
Chemical Type
Diversity of Fishes
Diversity of Benthos

*6. Freshwater lake (LMVD)---composite indicator based on
following 10 factors:

Mean Depth
Turbidity
TDS
Chemical Type
Shore Development
Spring Flooding
Standing Crop of Fishes
Standing Crop of Sport Fishes
Diversity of Fishes
Diversity of Benthos

*7. River swamp (LMVD)---composite indicator based on
following 6 factors:

Species Associations
Percent Forest Cover
Percent Flooded Annually
Groundcover Diversity
Percent coverage by Groundwater
Days Subject to River Overflow

*8. Non-river swamp (LMVD)---composite indicator based on following 5 factors:

> Species Associations
> Percent Forest Cover
> Percent **Flooded Annually**
> Groundcover Diversity
> Percent Coverage by Groundcover

9. Beaches and shores (Bureau of Reclamation)
10. Community alterations - freshwater, estuarine, ocean (Battelle Dredging Impact Assessment Method)
11. Wetlands (HUD)
12. Stream community downstream (Battelle Water Resources Project)

III. Water Quality

*1. pH (Battelle EES)
2. Odor intensity (SCS)
*3. Turbidity (Battelle EES)
*4. Suspended solids (Battelle Dredging Impact Assessment Method)
*5. Water temperature (Battelle EES)
6. Radioactivity (SCS)
*7. Dissolved oxygen (Battelle EES)
*8. Biochemical oxygen demand (Battelle EES)
9. Chemical oxygen demand (SCS)
10. Electrical conductance (SCS)
11. Calcium (SCS)
12. Magnesium (SCS)
13. Sodium (SCS)
14. Sodium absorption rate (SCS)
15. Acidity (SCS)
16. Alkalinity (SCS)
17. Chlorides (SCS)
18. Sulfates (SCS)
19. Bicarbonates (SCS)
*20. Dissolved solids (Battelle EES)
21. Nitrogen compounds (Battelle Water Resources Projects)
*22. Inorganic nitrogen (Battelle EES)
23. Phosphorus (Battelle Water Resources Projects)
*24. Inorganic phosphate (Battelle EES)
*25. Salinity (**Battelle** Dredging Impact Assessment Method)
26. Inorganic carbon (Battelle EES)
*27. Iron and manganese (Battelle Water Resources Projects)
*28. Toxic substances (Battelle EES)
29. **Heavy metals** (CERL)
*30. Pesticides (Battelle EES)
31. Oil (CERL)

32. Total coliforms (Battelle Water Resources Projects)
*33. Fecal coliforms (Battelle EES)
34. Fecal streptococcus (SCS)
*35. Stream assimilative capacity (Battelle EES)
36. Sedimentation (Battelle Water Resources Projects)
37. Thermal stratification (Battelle Water Resources Project)
38. Chemical reactions (Battelle Water Resources Projects)
39. Eutrophication (CERL)

IV. Water Quantity

1. Spring flooding (LMVD)
2. Percent of area flooded annually (LMVD)
3. Days subject to river overflow (LMVD)
*4. Stream flow variation (Battelle EES)
*5. Basin hydrologic loss (Battelle EES)
6. Interflow---groundwater (Battelle Dredging Impact Assessment Method)
7. Water uses and consumptive losses (SCS)
8. Aquifer safe yield (CERL)

V. Critical Community Relationships

1. Food web index (Battelle EES)
*2. Species diversity (Battelle EES)
3. Ecosystem productivity (Tulsa District)
4. Ecosystem diversity and stability (Tulsa District)

VI. Threatened and/or Endangered Species

1. Threatened and/or endangered species (Battelle EES)

VII. Pests

1. Pest species (Battelle EES)

AIR

I. Quality

*1. Carbon monoxide (Battelle EES)
*2. Hydrocarbons (Battelle EES)
*3. Oxides of nitrogen (Battelle EES)
4. Photochemical oxidants/ozone (Battelle EES)
5. **Sulfur oxides** (Battelle EES)
6. Ammonia (SCS)
7. Hydrogen sulfide (SCS)
8. Odor (CERL)
*9. Particulates (Battelle EES)

10. Pollen (SCS)
11. Smoke (SCS)
12. Visibility (SCS)
13. Hazardous toxicants (CERL)

II. Climatology

*1. Diffusion factor (CERL)
 2. Inversions (SCS)
 3. Air drainage (SCS)

HUMAN INTERFACE

I. Noise

*1. Noise (Battelle EES)
 2. Noise intensity (Battelle Dredging Impact Assessment Method)
 3. Noise duration (Battelle Dredging Impact Assessment Method)
 4. Noise frequency (SCS)
 5. **Physiological effects (CERL)**
 6. **Psychological effects (CERL)**
 7. Communication effects (CERL)
 8. Performance effects (CERL)
 9. Social behavior effects (CERL)

II. Esthetic

 1. Geological surface material (Battelle EES)
 2. Relief and topographic character (Battelle EES)
 3. Surface configuration (Battelle Dredging Impact Assessment Method)
*4. Width and alignment (Battelle EES)
 5. Visual quality of landscape (SCS)
 6. Open space and green belts (Bureau of Reclamation)
 7. Natural areas (Bureau of Reclamation)
 8. Other areas of natural beauty (Bureau of Reclamation)
 9. Diversity of vegetation type (Battelle EES)
*10. Variety within vegetation type (Battelle EES)
 11. Shore line vegetation (Battelle Dredging Impact Assessment Method)
 12. Upland vegetation (Battelle Dredging Impact Assessment Method)
 13. Terrestrial animals (Battelle Dredging Impact Assessment Method)
*14. Animals - domestic (Battelle EES)
*15. Native fauna (Battelle EES)
 16. Birdwatching (Battelle EES)
 17. Land/water interface (Battelle EES)

10

18. Water surface area (Battelle EES)
19. Wooded and geological shoreline (Battelle EES)
*20. Appearance of water (Battelle EES)
*21. Odor and floating materials (Battelle EES)
22. Aquatic animals (Battelle Dredging Impact Assessment Method)
23. Visibility (SCS)
*24. Odor and visual quality (Battelle EES)
*25. Sound (Battelle EES)

III. Historical

*1. Historical internal and external packages (Battelle EES)
2. Historical structures (HUD)

IV. Archeological

*1. Archeological internal and external packages (Battelle EES)
2. Archeological sites and structures (HUD)

TABLE 2: SUMMARY OF VARIABLES FOR ENVIRONMENTAL
QUALITY ACCOUNT

Terrestrial	Considered	Presented
I. Populations	18	6
II. Habitat/Land Use	17	5[a]
III. Land Quality/Soil Erosion	17	3
IV. Critical Community Relationships	5	1
V. Threatened and/or Endangered Species	1	0
VI. Pests	1	0
	59	15

Aquatic		
I. Population	11	9
II. Habitat	12	4[b]
III. Water Quality	39	15
IV. Water Quantity	8	2
V. Critical Community Relationships	4	1
VI. Threatened and/or Endangered Species	1	0
VII. Pests	1	0
	76	31

Air		
I. Quality	13	4
II. Climatology	3	1
	16	5

Human Interface		
I. Noise	9	1
II. Esthetics	25	8
III. Historical	2	1
IV. Archeological	2	1
	38	11
	189	62

a = three of the variables represent a composite of 25 individual variables

b = the four variables represent a composite of 29 individual variables

Account   **Category**   **Subcategory**   **Variable**

Environmental Quality Account

Terrestrial

Populations
- Crops
- Natural Vegetation
- Herbivorous Mammals
- Carnivorous Mammals
- Upland Game Birds
- Predatory Birds

Habitat/Land Use
- Bottomland Forest (1)
- Upland Forest (2)
- Open (nonforest) Lands (3)
- Drawdown Zone
- Land Use

Land Quality/Soil Erosion
- Soil Erosion
- Soil Chemistry
- Mineral Extraction

Critical Community Relationships
- Species Diversity

Aquatic

Populations
- Natural Vegetation
- Wetland Vegetation
- Zooplankton
- Phytoplankton
- Sport Fish
- Commercial Fisheries
- Intertidal Organisms
- Benthos/Epibenthos
- Waterfowl

Habitats
- Stream (4)
- Freshwater Lake (5)
- River Swamp (6)
- Nonriver Swamp (7)

Water Quality
- pH
- Turbidity
- Suspended Solids
- Water Temperature
- Dissolved Oxygen
- Biochemical Oxygen Demand
- Dissolved Solids
- Inorganic Nitrogen
- Inorganic Phosphate
- Salinity
- Iron and Manganese
- Toxic Substances
- Pesticides
- Fecal Coliforms
- Stream Assimilative Capacity

Water Quantity
- Stream Flow Variation
- Basin Hydrologic Loss

Critical Community Relationships
- Species Diversity

Air

Quality
- Carbon Monoxide
- Hydrocarbons
- Oxides of Nitrogen
- Particulates

Climatology
- Diffusion Factor

Noise
- Noise

Human Interface

Esthetics
- Width and Alignment
- Variety within Vegetation Type
- Animals—Domestic
- Native Fauna
- Appearance of Water
- Odor and Floating Materials
- Odor and Visual Quality
- Sound

Historical
- Historical Internal and External Packages

Archeological
- Archeological Internal and External Packages

Figure 1. Structure of the Environmental Quality Account

13

(1) Bottomland forest represents a composite consideration of the following 11 parameters: species associations, percent mast-bearing trees, percent coverage by understory, diversity of understory, percent coverage by ground over, diversity of groundcover, number of trees > 16 in. (or 18 in.) dbh per acre, percent of trees > 16 in. (or 18 in.) dbh, frequency of inundation, edge (quantity) and edge (quality).

(2) Upland forest represents a composite consideration of the following 10 parameters: species associations, percent mast-bearing trees, percent coverage of understory, diversity of understory, percent coverage of groundcover, diversity of groundcover, number of trees $\geq$ 16 in. dbh/acre, percent of trees $\geq$ 16 in. dbh, quantity of edge and mean distance to edge.

(3) Open (non-forest) lands represent a composite consideration of the following 4 parameters: land use, diversity of land use, quantity of edge, mean distance to edge.

(4) Stream represents a composite consideration of the following 8 parameters: sinuosity, dominant centrarchids, mean low water width, turbidity, total dissolved solids, chemical type, diversity of fishes and diversity of benthos.

(5) Freshwater lake represents a composite consideration of the following 10 parameters: mean depth, turbidity, total dissolved solids, chemical type, shore development, spring flooding above vegetation line, standing crop of fishes, standing crop of sport fish, diversity of fishes, and diversity of benthos.

(6) River swamp represents a composite consideration of the following 6 parameters: species associations, percent forest cover, percent flooded annually, groundcover diversity, percent coverage of groundcover, and days subject to river overflow.

(7) Non-river swamp represents a composite consideration of the following 5 parameters: species associations, percent forest cover, percent flooded annually, groundcover diversity and percent coverage by groundcover.

TERRESTRIAL VARIABLES

ACCOUNT: ENVIRONMENTAL QUALITY

CATEGORY: TERRESTRIAL

SUBCATEGORY: POPULATIONS

VARIABLE: CROPS

Definition and Measurement of Baseline Conditions: Crops
include both grain and forage species. Substantial data on
both the area covered by the various types of farming (irrigated, dry, grazed) and the productivity of these areas are
generally available and facilitate the evaluation of this
parameter.

The value function for crops is linear. The horizontal
axis is the percent of the total arable land within the project boundaries which is cultivated. The total arable land
is defined at 100 percent on the horizontal axis. To obtain
the percent "with" or "without" a proposed project, the concept of magnitude modified by a measure of quality for that
magnitude is used. The magnitude for crops is the area in
acres for each type of farming- irrigated, dry, and grazed.
The quality modifier is a weighted estimate of net annual
fresh weight production. The modifier is weighted on a 0 to
1 scale as follows:

Modifer Value	Production
1.0	8,000 lb/acre/yr
0.75	4,000 lb/acre/yr
0.50	2,000 lb/acre/yr
0.25	1,000 lb/acre/yr
0	0 lb/acre/yr

Prediction of Impacts: Net annual production is determined
for each farming type and then assigned a modifier value
using the above scale. The fractional quality modifier
obtained is multiplied by the magnitude, in acres, of the
farming type to give a modified acreage. Summing the modified acreages for the farming types, dividing this sum by
the total arable acreage ("without" the project), and then
multiplying the quotient by 100 gives the weighted percent
to use in the value function:

$$\text{Parameter Estimate} = \sum_{1}^{N} \frac{(\text{Acres of Farming Type x K})}{\text{Total Arable Land}} \times 100$$

where

    N = number of farming types
    K = weighted productivity

16

Functional Curve (Battelle Environmental Evaluation System, 1972)

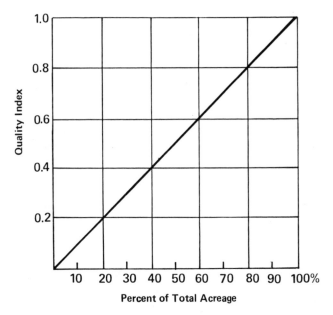

Remarks: This value function does not distinquish between forage or grain crops. Further, the modifier values may alter with each type of farming - irrigated, dry, and grazed.

Data Sources:

Battelle Environmental Evaluation System (1972).

References:

Klopatek and Risser (1977).

ACCOUNT: ENVIRONMENTAL QUALITY

CATEGORY: TERRESTRIAL

SUBCATEGORY: POPULATIONS

VARIABLE: NATURAL VEGETATION

Definition and Measurement of Baseline Conditions: Natural
vegetation, species adapted to the climatic and edaphic
regimes of a region, supports the autotrophic production of
food resources for biotic communities. Changes in species
composition or total biomass may reduce significantly food
resources for heterotrophs and encourage changes in the
structural and functional attributes of the ecosystem through
erosion, reduction of fertility and invasion of undesirable
plant species.
    Measurement involves determining the acreages of land
use types within project boundaries.
    The concept of a magnitude multiplied by a quality
modifier is used in this value function. The magnitude is a
measurement of area and the qualifier is a weighted estimate
of net primary production. To maintain the 100% limit, the
modifier must be given a 0 to 1 weight. The available area
for natural vegetation within the project boundaries is the
total amount of nonarable land (exclusive of urban, industrial
and residential). This area is 100% on the value function.

Prediction of Impacts: To determine the actual values for a
site with or without the project, the area of each type of
natural vegetation habitat is determined in addition to net
annual primary production for that habitat. The net production is connected to a fraction using 0 to 1 scale. The
fraction obtained is multiplied by the area of the habitat
type. Summing these values for all the habitat types gives
a weighted acreage which, when divided by the total nonarable acreage, gives the percent value with or without the
project.

$$\text{Parameter Estimate} = \sum_{1}^{N} \frac{(\text{Acres of vegetation type x K})}{\text{Total nonarable land}} \times 100$$

where

    N = number of categories
    K = weighted productivity (See Crops Variable)

Functional Curve (Battelle Environmental Evaluation System,
1972) (on next page)

18

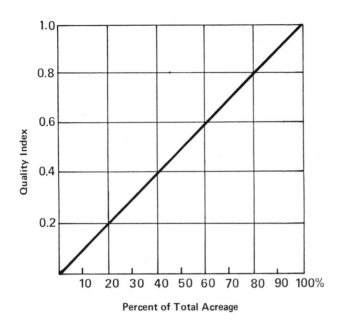

Percent of Total Acreage

Remarks: The value function may be given as percent acreage of vegetation type total nonarable land. Individual projects would have to evaluate the desirability of these percentages.

The function curve presented above assumes that 100% coverage represents top environmental quality; however, bare ground and clearings of sparse vegetation may be highly important to some animal species.

Data Source:

Battelle Environmental Evaluation System (1972).

References:

Lindsey, Schmelz, and Nichols (1969).

ACCOUNT: ENVIRONMENTAL QUALITY

CATEGORY: TERRESTRIAL

SUBCATEGORY: POPULATIONS

VARIABLE: HERBIVOROUS MAMMALS

Definition and Measurement of Baseline Conditions: Herbivores
including cattle, horses, sheep and other livestock as well as
deer, elk and other wild herbivores are dominant plant consumers of many terrestrial systems, as these organisms feed
directly on living plants or plant remains. Changes in their
density or in the carrying capacity may result in significant
impact on the productivity of the environment.

Ultimate capacity is used in evaluating the magnitude of
impact of predicted changes in these populations. The ultimate capacity defines the number of herbivores that could be
supported if they consumed all the net annual plant production.
Herbivores normally consume only 50 to 60% of the net annual,
above-ground production of plants. This phenomenon is referred
to as the carrying capacity, which describes the maximum number,
biomass, etc. that an ecosystem supports on a sustained basis.
The remaining 40 to 50% of annual plant production represents
the regenerating portions of the plants. Thus, maximum production is attained at 50 to 60% of the ultimate capacity of
the land within the project boundaries. When this range is
exceeded, the reproductive capacity of the system is disturbed
and production declines. At values less than optimum, the
value function also declines, indicating that the full potential of the system is not being utilized.

The ultimate capacity of the land is determined both with
and without the project. The number of herbivores, by species,
occurring within the boundaries without the project is obtained.
These data are converted to animal units (AU), a standard
measure based on the food consumption of a cow (9,600 lbs/yr).
Net annual production in pounds per acre is determined for
each habitat type. Dividing the AU requirements in pounds per
year, by the net annual plant production in pounds per year
for each habitat type gives the number of acres of each habitat
type needed to support one AU:

$$\frac{\text{Acres of habitat}}{\text{AU}} = \frac{\text{AU}}{\text{Net Plant Production}}$$

AU = lb/year
Net Plant Production = lb/acre/year

Dividing the number of acres of each habitat type (without
the project) by the number of acres required to support one
AU gives the ultimate capacity in AU for each habitat. Summing

20

the carrying capacities for the several habitat gives the ultimate capacity for the total project area and is the number equated with 100% of the value function.

$$\text{Ultimate Capacity} = \sum_{1}^{N} \frac{\text{Acres of Habitat Type}}{\text{Acres of Habitat/AU}}$$

N = number of habitat types

Dividing the total AU of the project by the ultimate capacity and multiplying by 100 gives the percent ultimate capacity without the project:

$$\text{Parameter Function} = \frac{\text{Total AU}}{\text{Ultimate Capacity}} \times 100$$

<u>Prediction of Impacts</u>: Repeating the procedures, using any changes in area, annual production, and number of AU caused by the construction and operation of the project, gives the ultimate capacity, number of AU, and the percent of ultimate capacity these AU comprise with the project.

<u>Functional Curve</u> (Battelle Environmental Evaluation System, 1972)

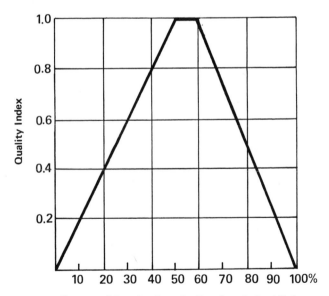

Percent of Carrying Capacity Based on Animal Units

21

Remarks: With this value function, the animal units (AU) and requirements can be expected to vary among species. This assessment does not evaluate the impact of small herbivores.

Data Source:

Battelle Environmental Evaluation System (1972).

References:

Stoddard and Smith (1955).
Heady (1975).

ACCOUNT: ENVIRONMENTAL QUALITY

CATEGORY: TERRESTRIAL

SUBCATEGORY: POPULATIONS

VARIABLE: CARNIVOROUS MAMMALS

Definition and Measurement of Baseline Conditions: Carnivores, or secondary consumers, are heterotrophs deriving their energy indirectly from the producer via way of the herbivore. This group would include the predatory mammals, i.e., fox, raccoon, coyote, mink, badger, bear and lion. Changes in their density or in the carrying capacity may result in significant impact on the structure and function of the environment. (U.S. Department of the Army, 1975).

The number and species of carnivorous mammals that reside, breed and capture their food within the project area should be determined. The change in the amount of available habitat (breeding and feeding) must be ascertained to estimate the number of carnivores which the existing habitat will support once the activity is completed or the project becomes operational.

When feasible, a direct census of predatory mammals inhabiting the project area should be determined. Indirect methods of numbers may be obtained from trapping efforts. Changes in acreage used for breeding, care of young, and feeding can be estimated from before and after overlays prepared from aerial photographs. Size use areas can also be estimated, and for common carnivorous mammals, the breeding and feeding habitats can be combined and a direct proportion established between the mammal population and available habitat. The following equation reflects this relationship:

$$\text{Future Population} = \frac{\text{Present Population} \times \text{(Future Habitat Acreage)}}{\text{Present Habitat Acreage}}$$

Prediction of Impacts: The change in numbers of carnivorous mammals as related to a particular activity and location suggest a change in habitat quality for such species within the area.

Functional Curve: None available

Remarks: Assessment methodology is oversimplified and census data are difficult to obtain.

Data Sources:

U.S. Department of the Army (1975).

References:

Schwartz and Schwartz (1959).
Thomas et al (1976).

23

ACCOUNT: ENVIRONMENTAL QUALITY

CATEGORY: TERRESTRIAL

SUBCATEGORY: POPULATIONS

VARIABLE: UPLAND GAME BIRDS

Definition and Measurement of Baseline Conditions: Upland
game birds refers to a variety of species of marketable birds
that are hunted but are not associated with water, e.g., quail,
turkey, prairie chicken, pheasant, and grouse. These birds
are important both as a source of recreation and food for man
and as an indicator of inter-year variability and productivity
of the habitats they use. While small mammals, arthropods,
reptiles, song birds, and others may also live in these same
habitats, data on the density and area used can be obtained
specifically for the upland game birds. This fact, along
with their value as game animals, make them an excellent
indicator of environmental conditions.
    The quality increases as the percentage of total suitable
habitat acreage for upland game birds increases. The magnitude
measured is the habitat area, and the total available area
within the project boundaries is equated with 100 percent.
The actual magnitude "with" or "without" the project is the
area inhabited, and its quality modifier is the weighted
annual harvest of birds. A scale from 0 to 1 is used:

$$
\begin{array}{ll}
1.00 & \text{Maximum possible harvest} \\
0.75 & \\
0.50 & \\
0.25 & \\
0 & \text{No harvest}
\end{array}
$$

    Using past harvest records, the maximum possible annual
harvest can be calculated. These harvests which are reported
during the years of record for all the upland game species
occurring within the project boundaries are averaged to give
the total maximum annual harvest. For newly introduced species
not yet at their maximum level, an estimate of that level must
be made. This number is equated with 1.0 on the modifier
scale. The annual harvest for the year nearest the environmental analysis is divided by the maximum, the resulting
quotient being the modifier to be multiplied by the actual
inhabited area. This product, divided by the total possible
habitat is the parameter estimate "without" the project:

$$
\text{Parameter Estimate} = \frac{\text{Area Inhabited x K}}{\text{Maximum Habitat Area}} \text{ x } 100
$$

24

where

K = weighted annual harvest

Prediction of Impacts: Predicted changes in the area inhabited (including habitat inundated) and in the annual
harvest caused by the construction and operation of the
project are used to determine the parameter value "with" the
project.

Functional Curve (Battelle Environmental Evaluation System,
1972)

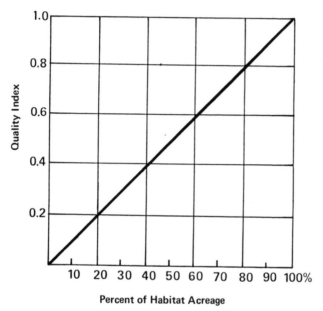

Remarks: In this assessment, caution must be taken when using
harvest records, as such records may be variable and of unknown
accuracy.

Data Sources:

Battelle Environmental Evaluation System (1972).

References:

Battelle Dredging Impact Assessment Method (1974).
Brookhaven (1969).

ACCOUNT: ENVIRONMENTAL QUALITY

CATEGORY: TERRESTRIAL

SUBCATEGORY: POPULATIONS

VARIABLE: PREDATORY BIRDS

Definition and Measurement of Baseline Conditions: Birds of
prey are flesh eaters and obtain their food primarily by
hunting, and consuming invertebrates, other birds, small
mammals, reptiles, amphibians, and fishes.   Common birds in
this group (Order Falconiformes and Strigiformes) are hawks,
owls, and vultures.   Less common are eagles, ospreys, and
some of the falcons (U.S. Department of the Army, 1975).

The number and species of birds of prey that nest or
capture their food within the project area should be determined.   The change in the amount of available habitat (nesting and/or feeding) must be ascertained to estimate the
numbers of birds which the existing habitat will support once
the activity is completed or the project becomes operational.

When feasible, a direct census of common birds of prey
inhabiting the area is desirable.   Changes in acreage of
nesting and feeding habitats can be obtained from before and
after overlays prepared from aerial photographs.   Size of use-
areas can be determined, and for common birds of prey, the
nesting and feeding habitats can be combined and a direct
proportion established between the bird population and the
number of acres of available habitat.   The following equation
reflects this relationship:

$$\text{Future Population} = \frac{\text{Present Population X (Future Habitat Acreage)}}{\text{Present Habitat Acreage}}$$

The change in numbers of birds of prey as related to a
particular activity and location suggest a change in habitat
quality for such species within the area.

Functional Curve: None available

Remarks: Census data on the number and species of predatory
birds that nest or capture their food within the project
area are difficult to obtain.

Data Sources:

U.S. Department of the Army (1975).

References:

Hooper, Crawford, and Harlow (1976).

26

ACCOUNT: ENVIRONMENTAL QUALITY

CATEGORY: TERRESTRIAL

SUBCATEGORY: HABITATS/LAND USE

VARIABLE: BOTTOMLAND FOREST

Definition and Measurement of Baseline Conditions: Bottomland forests are composed of a variety of species which inhabit floodplain areas and are significant habitats for
animals. Evaluation of this habitat type is based on the
composite of eleven key parameters. (Lower Mississippi
Valley Division, 1976). These parameters were identified
in a joint study effort between biologists at the Lower
Mississippi Valley Division and WES. Approximately 20
persons participated in the study. Key outputs from the
study were: (1) the identification of parameters associated
with three terrestrial habitat types (bottomland forest,
upland forest, and open lands) and four aquatic habitat types
(stream, freshwater lake, river swamp, and non-river swamp);
(2) the assignment of relative importance weights to the
identified parameters for each habitat type; and (3) the
presentation of functional curves for each identified parameter. Evaluation of field applications of the outputs is
under current study.
    The eleven parameters for bottomland forests are:

1. Species associations -- dominant trees species composition.

2. Percent mast-bearing trees -- estimated percent
   composition of mast-producing species ($\geq$ 10 in. dbh).

3. Percent coverage by understory -- average percent of
   habitat type covered by understory ($\geq$ 12 ft. tall)
   species.

4. Diversity of understory -- average number of understory species per unit area.

5. Percent coverage by groundcover -- average percent
   of ground covered by groundcover (herb) species.

6. Diversity of groundcover -- average number of groundcover species per unit area.

7. Number of trees > 16 in. (or 18 in.) dbh per acre --
   estimated number of large living trees per acre of
   habitat.

27

8. <u>Percent of trees > 16 in. (or 18 in.) dbh</u> -- estimated percent composition of large trees in proportion to all other living trees (> 6 in. dbh) within the habitat.

9. <u>Frequency of inundation</u> -- an estimate (for bottomland forest) of the recurrence frequency of flooding which occurs over a large proportion of the habitat area.

10. <u>Edge (quantity)</u> -- using a grid overlay of the study area, determine the number of grids in which "edge" occurs as a percentage of the total number of grids.

11. <u>Edge (quality)</u> -- using a numbered grid overlay of the study area and a table of random numbers, determine the average distance to "edge."

Each functional curve shown below was developed to transform raw data into an index value between 0.0 and 1.0. Each parameter is assigned a weight which accounts for its relative importance in describing habitat quality. The weights for the eleven parameters are as follows:

	PARAMETER	WEIGHT
1.	Species Associations	17
2.	Percent Mast-Bearing Trees	12
3.	Percent Coverage by Understory	8
4.	Diversity of Understory	7
5.	Percent Coverage by Groundcover	7
6.	Diversity of Groundcover	6
7.	Number of Trees > 18" dbh/acre	8
8.	Percent of Trees > 18" dbh	6
9.	Frequency of Inundation	9
10.	Quantity of Edge	11
11.	Mean Distance to Edge	9

The product of these two terms yields a weighted index value for each parameter. From these data a weighted mean is calculated which represents the quality of that particular habitat. The procedure is repeated to arrive at an estimate of the quality of each major habitat type occurring within the project area for each alternative plan.

<u>Prediction of Impacts</u>: The effects of various alternative plans of development can then be compared by applying the quality values to acreage of habitats for each alternative considered. For example, the acreage of each habitat multiplied by its quality value yields a final habitat value. The values thus assigned to the various habitats within the study area are

summed to give an evaluation of the whole study area for each project alternative, including the "no action" alternative.

<u>Functional Curve:</u>   See the following 11 curves.

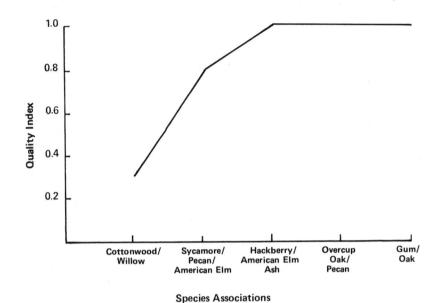

Species Associations

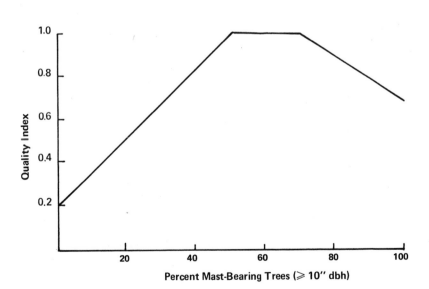

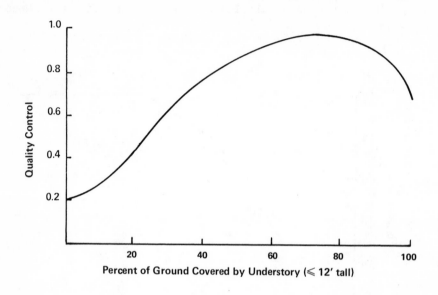

Percent of Ground Covered by Understory (≤ 12′ tall)

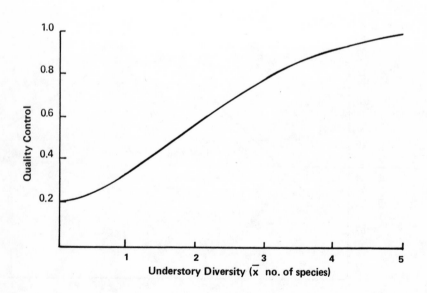

Understory Diversity (x̄ no. of species)

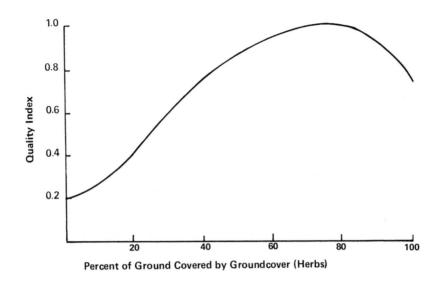

Percent of Ground Covered by Groundcover (Herbs)

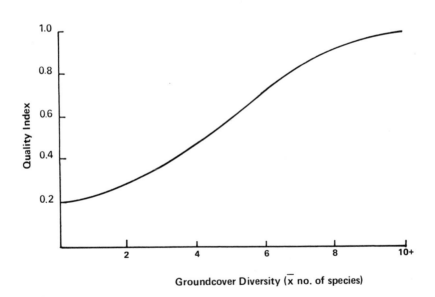

Groundcover Diversity ($\bar{x}$ no. of species)

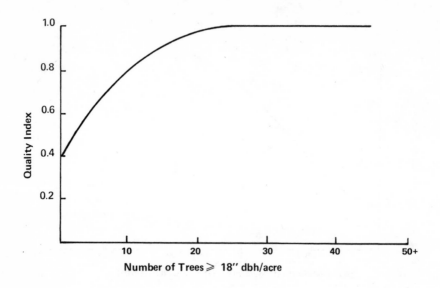

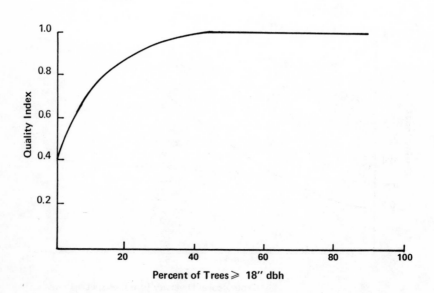

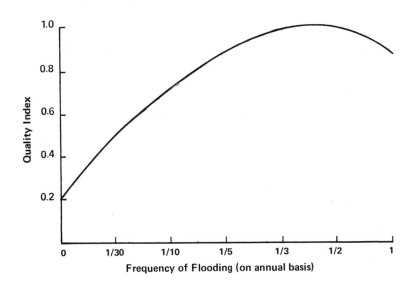

Frequency of Flooding (on annual basis)

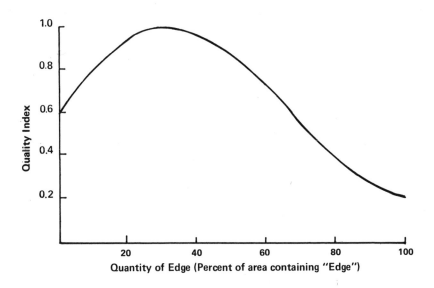

Quantity of Edge (Percent of area containing "Edge")

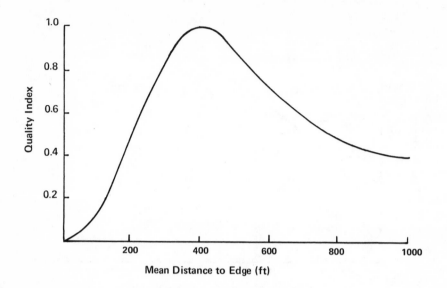

Remarks: The index values and weights used in this assessment may be subject to alteration among geographical areas.

Data Sources:

Lower Mississippi Valley Division (1976).

References:

Glasgow and Noble (1971).
Hosner and Minckler(1963).

ACCOUNT: ENVIRONMENTAL QUALITY

CATEGORY: TERRESTRIAL

SUBCATEGORY: HABITATS/LAND USE

VARIABLE: UPLAND FOREST

Definition and Measurement of Baseline Conditions: Upland forests are composed of a variety of plant species which inhabit areas of relatively high elevations that are not subject to flooding, as distinguished from forest in flood-plain areas.

Evaluation of this habitat type is based on the composite of ten key parameters. (Lower Mississippi Valley Division, 1976). These parameters were identified in a joint study effort between biologists at the Lower Mississippi Valley Division and WES. Approximately 20 persons participated in the study. Key outputs from the study were: (1) the identi-fication of parameters associated with three terrestrial habitat types (bottomland forest, upland forest, and open lands) and four aquatic habitat types (stream, freshwater lake, river swamp, and non-river swamp); (2) the assignment of relative importance weights to the identified parameters for each habitat type; and (3) the presentation of functional curves for each identified parameter. Evaluation of field applications of the outputs is under current study.

The ten parameters for upland forests and their importance weights are:

PARAMETER	WEIGHT
1. Species Associations	17
2. Percent Mast-Bearing Trees	15
3. Percent Coverage of Understory	9
4. Diversity of Understory	9
5. Percent Coverage of Groundcover	7
6. Diversity of Groundcover	8
7. Number of trees $\geq$ 16" dbh/acre	8
8. Percent of trees $\geq$ 16" dbh	6
9. Quantity of Edge	12
10. Mean Distance to Edge	9

Prediction of Impacts: These parameters are defined under Bottomland Forest in the Terrestrial/Habitats/Land Use cate-gory. For prediction of impacts, see discussion for Bottom-land Forest in the Terrestrial/Habitats/Land Use Category.

Functional Curve: See the following ten curves.

35

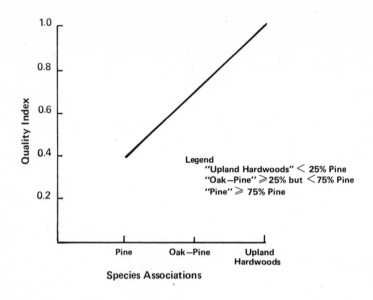

Legend
"Upland Hardwoods" < 25% Pine
"Oak—Pine" ≥ 25% but < 75% Pine
"Pine" ≥ 75% Pine

Species Associations

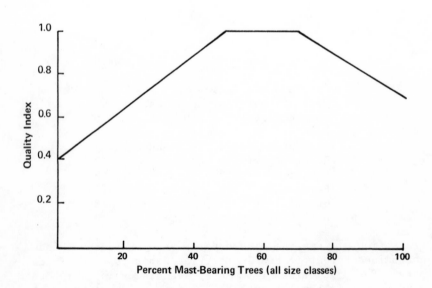

36

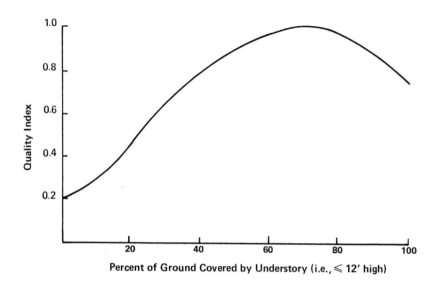

Percent of Ground Covered by Understory (i.e., ≤ 12' high)

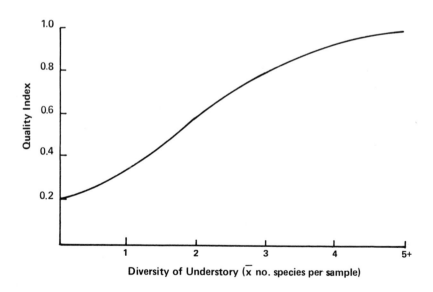

Diversity of Understory ($\overline{x}$ no. species per sample)

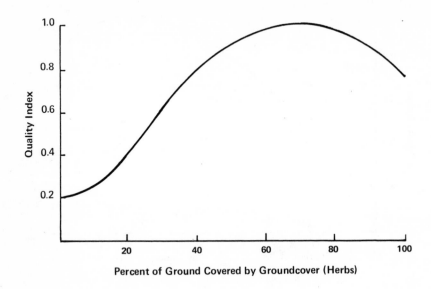

Percent of Ground Covered by Groundcover (Herbs)

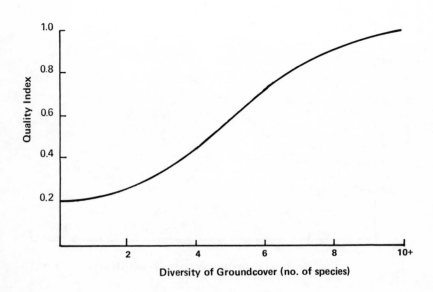

Diversity of Groundcover (no. of species)

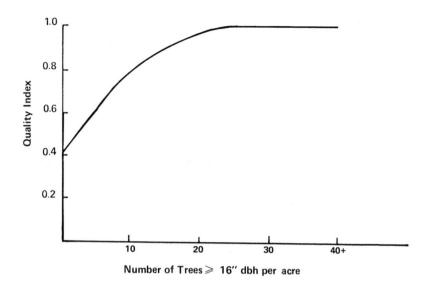

Number of Trees ≥ 16″ dbh per acre

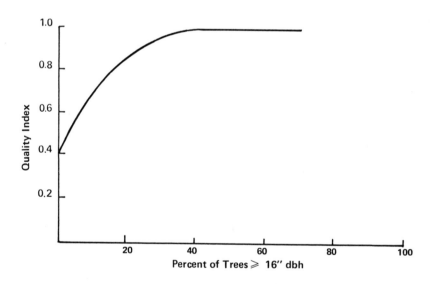

Percent of Trees ≥ 16″ dbh

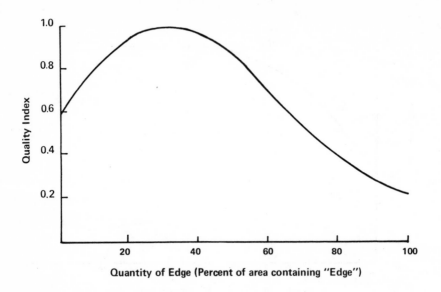

Quantity of Edge (Percent of area containing "Edge")

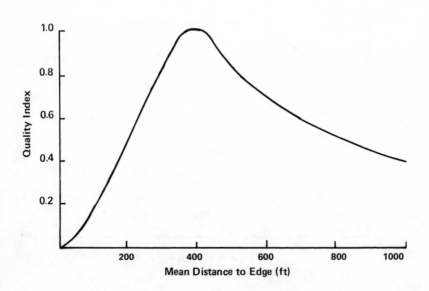

Mean Distance to Edge (ft)

40

Remarks: Index values and weights may need to be altered among geographical regions. A standard equation should be applied to all assessments of upland forests.

Data Source:

Lower Mississippi Valley Division (1976).

References:

Horn (1974).

ACCOUNT: ENVIRONMENTAL QUALITY

CATEGORY: TERRESTRIAL

SUBCATEGORY: HABITATS/LAND USE

VARIABLE: OPEN (NON-FOREST) LANDS

Definition and Measurement of Baseline Conditions: Open
(non-forest) lands are areas characterized by grasses, forbes,
or crops, which provide habitat for animals. Environmental
parameters (temperature, evaporation, soil type, and moisture
content) are important to the maintenance of such habitats
although the extant conditions of these parameters vary among
geographic regions. Evaluation of this habitat type is based
on the composite of four key parameters. (Lower Mississippi
Valley Division, 1976). These parameters were identified in
a joint study effort between biologists at the Lower Mississippi
Valley Division and WES. Approximately 20 persons participated
in the study. Key outputs from the study were: (1) the
identification of parameters associated with three terrestrial
habitat types (bottomland forest, upland forest, and open lands)
and four aquatic habitat types (stream, freshwater lake, river
swamp, and non-river swamp); (2) the assignment of relative
importance weights to the identified parameters for each
habitat type; and (3) the presentation of functional curves
for each identified parameter. Evaluation of field applications
of the outputs is under current study.

The four parameters for open lands are:
1. Land use -- the type of use.
2. Diversity of land use -- the variety of
   used within the area.
3. Quantity of edge -- see definition under
   Bottomland Forest in Terrestrial/Habitats
   category.
4. Mean distance to edge -- same as 3 above.

The importance weights assigned to those four parameters
are as follows:

PARAMETER	WEIGHT
1. Land Use	30
2. Diversity of Land Use	15
3. Quantity of Edge	30
4. Mean Distance to Edge	25

Prediction of Impacts: For prediction of impacts, see
discussion for Bottomland Forest in the Terrestrial/Habitats/
Land Use Category.

<u>Functional Curve</u>: See the following four curves.

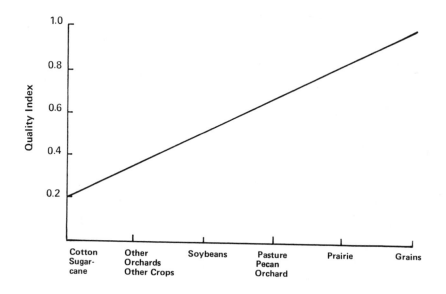

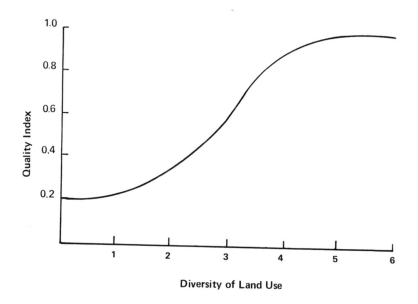

Diversity of Land Use

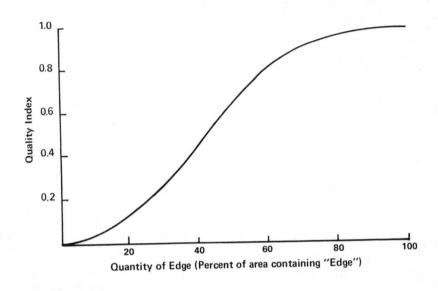

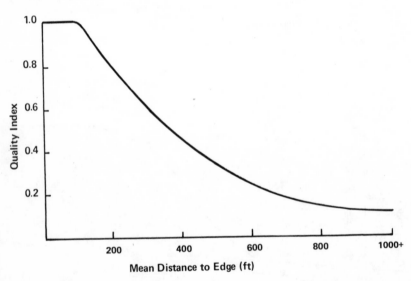

Remarks: The predilection with quantity of edge and mean distance to edge is likely most important to wildlife and may exert too much emphasis in this assessment.

Data Sources:

Lower Mississippi Valley Division (1976).

References:

Risser (1975).

44

ACCOUNT: ENVIRONMENTAL QUALITY

CATEGORY: TERRESTRIAL

SUBCATEGORY: HABITATS/LAND USE

VARIABLE: DRAWDOWN ZONE

Definition and Measurement of Baseline Conditions: The drawdown zone is defined as the terrestrial-aquatic interface
which may be exposed or inundated periodically due to water-
level fluctuations.   As water input seldom coincides with
water output, changes in water volume occur; the magnitude
of that change is dependent upon the purpose of the water
project.   Water projects designed for channel maintenance
or water supply seldom have large volume changes; thus, the
potential for creating a drawdown zone is slight.   Flood
control projects do have seasonal fluctuations in water levels
large enough to form drawdown zones.   Shallow water areas
subject to drawdown contribute significantly to aquatic productivity and as habitat for species of plants and animals
(Keith, 1975).

Prediction of Impacts: For water resource projects where
drawdown zones occur, several variables are of significance,
including topography, extent of drawdown, frequency of
occurrence, duration, and time of year drawdown is anticipated.
To avoid the unwarranted complexity of handling these multiple
variables, two have been selected for incorporation into the
drawdown functional curve shown below.   These are the intensity
of drawdown and the frequency of occurrence within the project
area.   Intensity is represented by feet units and by a subjective scale from natural to drawdown.   The quality index is
shown to decrease with both increasing intensity and increasing
frequency.

   Functional Curve (see following page)

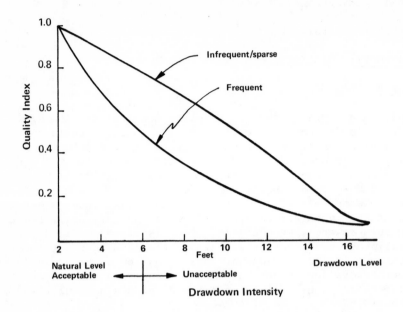

Remarks: As indicated, other features important to this assessment include topography, duration of drawdown and the time of year. For each project, these components should be considered as part of the assessment.

Data Sources:

Keith (1975).

References:

Bell and Johnson (1974).
Ortolano (1973).
Pierce, Frey and Yawn (1963).
Wistendahl and Lewis (1972).

ACCOUNT: ENVIRONMENTAL QUALITY

CATEGORY: TERRESTRIAL

SUBCATEGORY: HABITATS/LAND USE

VARIABLE: LAND USE

Definition and Measurement of Baseline Conditions: Land is a valuable resource and compatibility of the various kinds of land uses is important toward maintenance of environmental quality. This variable is evaluated for land use within the boundaries "without" the project by recognizing six land uses and ranking them in order of their compatibility with each other. "With" the project there may be changes in this baseline pattern. The location of the project or resulting developments may be very important in determining the direction and magnitude of this change. Thus, to maintain or prevent undesirably large decreases in environmental quality, consideration must be given to the location of various developments.

There are six basic kinds of land use which are ranked in order of compatibility and weighted according to their rank:

CATEGORY	WEIGHT
Industrial	0
Commercial	0.2
Residential	0.4
Agricultural	0.6
Managed forest	0.8
Natural	1.0

Natural land use is most different from industrial land use. The other categories are ranked in reference to these two extremes. Using magnitudes as a measure of area, the total land acreage within the project boundaries is represented as 100 percent on the value function. The acreage within the project boundaries is represented as 100 percent on the value function. The acreage for each type of land use is determined and multiplied by the weight for that type. In cases where acreages are of two or more types are combined and the area for each component cannot be determined, an intermediate weight is assigned. For example, if industrial and commercial acreages are combined, then that combination is given a weight of 0.1. The sum of weighted acreages divided by the total acreage and then multiplied by 100 is the value for the parameter "with" or "without" the project:

$$\text{Parameter Estimate } = \sum_{1}^{N} \frac{(\text{Land Use Area x K})}{\text{Total Land Use}}$$

where

N = number of land uses
K = weighted land use types

Prediction of Impacts: Land inundated by a project should be subtracted from the appropriate land use type. However, the total land area used as the divisor should not be similarly reduced in the evaluation "with" the project. This insures that the impact of the lost area is fully assessed.

Functional Curve (Battelle Environmental Evaluation System, 1972)

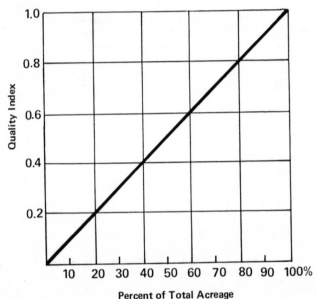

Remarks: The categories of Residential and Agricultural are weighted similarly; however, Industrial and Commercial are considered less similar to each although this concept may be altered with each project.

Data Sources:

Battelle Environmental Evaluation System (1972).

References:

None

ACCOUNT: ENVIRONMENTAL CATEGORY

CATEGORY: TERRESTRIAL

SUBCATEGORY: LAND QUALITY/SOIL EROSION

VARIABLE: SOIL EROSION

Definition and Measurement of Baseline Conditions: Erosion is
defined as the process through which soil particles are dis-
lodged and transported to other locations by the actions of
water and/or wind. Erosion can be altered as a result of
changes in land uses and associated vegetative cover. Soils
of almost all types are held in place on slopes by vegetative
cover and its associated root system. Removal of this cover
exposes the soil to the erosive forces of water and wind.
Erosion is intensely destructive. First, the site itself may
be denuded of its most productive top soils and/or may be
gullied to the extent that it becomes almost totally unpro-
ductive, often to the point of posing a physical barrier to
other activities. Second, the streams and lakes which receive the attendant sediment loads may be affected not only
in terms of general water quality, but also relative to the
overall ecosystem. After erosive forces have been at work,
the landscape is barren and aesthetically unappealing. Major
variables affecting erosion are soil composition or texture,
degree of slope, uninterrupted length of slope, nature add
extent of vegetative cover, and intensity and frequency of
exposure to the eroding forces.

The Soil Conservation Service will be the primary source
of information. Most soil-loss or soil-erosion equations are
based upon models that represent interrelationships among the
various factors affecting soil erosion. One model developed
for agricultural cropland, but subject to modification for
other vegetative types is (U.S. Department of the Army, 1975):

$$A = RKLSCP$$

where

    A = computer soil loss per unit area
    R = rainfall factor
    K = soil-erodibility factor
    L = slope-length factor
    S = slope-gradient factor
    C = crop-management factor
    P = erosion-control-practice factor.

Prediction of Impacts: Prediction of the impact of a potential
project would primarily involve calculation of the changes in
soil erosion resulting from the project. The soil erosion

49

equation listed above can be utilized to estimate anticipated soil erosion with the potential project.

The functional curve shown below is based on the premise that increasing the soil erosion is undesirable from the standpoint of environmental quality (Battelle Environmental Evaluation System, 1972). The following descriptors are appropriate to the functional curve:

Sediment Yield acre-ft/sq mi/year	Descriptor
0	None
0.2	Negligible
0.5	Slight
1.0	Moderate
> 3.0	Excessive

Functional Curve

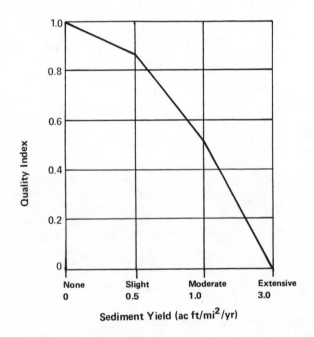

Sediment Yield (ac ft/mi^2/yr)

Remarks: Since soil erosion varies with a variety of factors, the erosion from sub-areas within each watershed in the project area needs to be determined.

Data Sources:

    Battelle Environmental Evaluation System (1972).
    U.S. Department of the Army (1975).

References:
    Environmental Protection Agency (1973).

ACCOUNT: ENVIRONMENTAL QUALITY

CATEGORY: TERRESTRIAL

SUBCATEGORY: LAND QUALITY/SOIL EROSION

VARIABLE: SOIL CHEMISTRY

Definition and Measurement of Baseline Conditions: Soil
chemistry refers to various chemical constituents in the soils
of a potential project area that could be potentially introduced into surface watercourses as a result of soil erosion.
The key concern is that these chemicals in surface watercourses could lead to reductions in environmental quality.
Examples of these chemicals include nutrients such as nitrogen
and phosphorus, metals such as iron, and pesticides. (Thomas,
1972).
     Measurement of this variable would basically involve the
same procedures as utilized for soil erosion, with additional
consideration being given to chemical constituents of the
soil and the potential for solubilization of these chemical
constituents once they are transported or found in the surface
watercourse.

Prediction of Impacts: Prediction of the impacts of this
variable would be basically the same as for prediction of
soil erosion impacts, with the added feature of considering
the potential for various soil chemicals to be introduced
into surface watercourses. The interdisciplinary team would
have to exercise professional judgment with regard to the
chemicals of concern, the quantities which would be potentially
introduced to the surface watercourse, and their potential
for causing undesirable impacts on water quality. The
functional curve shown below reflects the necessary qualitative
judgments.

Functional Curve

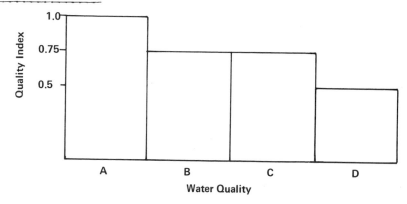

51

A = Water quality in existing environment not deterior-
ated by soil chemistry in watershed; no pronounced
deterioration is anticipated from project.

B = Water quality in existing environment not deterior-
ated by soil chemistry in watershed; some deterioration is anticipated from project despite construction methods to minimize impacts.

C = Water quality in existing environment is deterior-
ated by soil chemistry in watershed; no additional
deterioration is anticipated from project.

D = Water quality in existing environment is deterior-
ated by soil chemistry in watershed; some additional
deterioration is anticipated from project despite
construction methods to minimize impacts.

Remarks: Particular attention due to be given to nutrients,
metals and pesticides. Professional judgment will be required in considering both existing and potential water
quality deterioration.

Data Sources:

Thomas (1972).

References:

Environmental Protection Agency (1973).

ACCOUNT: ENVIRONMENTAL QUALITY

CATEGORY: TERRESTRIAL

SUBCATEGORY: LAND QUALITY/SOIL EROSION

VARIABLE: MINERAL EXTRACTION

Definition and Measurement of Baseline Conditions: Development of water resources project in an area having potentially
valuable geological resources such as sand, gravel, coal,
petroleum, and/or precious metals may conflict with future
recovery of these resources. Improving techniques of resource recovery and processing, and diminishing natural resources, present the possibility that mineral deposits which
currently have lower than acceptable value might become
valuable in the future. This variable is important relative
to potential site location as well as precluding future development of the mineral resources.
    Aggregation of information on the existing mineral
resources in the potential project area would be necessary.
Consideration should be given to the previous history of
mineral extraction in the area, as well as the potential for
future development of the resources.

Prediction of Impacts: Prediction of the impact of a water
resources project would require professional judgment by the
interdisciplinary team relative to the extent to which mineral
extraction would be precluded as a result of the project.

Functional Curve (Voorhees, 1975)

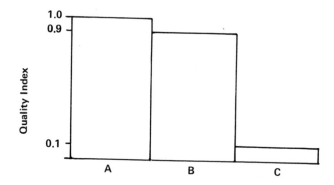

A = There is no indication of potentially valuable
    deposits on or near the site.
B = There are potentially valuable deposits on or
    adjacent to the site, but there are no plans
    for extraction.

53

C = There are potentially valuable deposits on or
adjacent to the site. There is a high likelihood
that they will be developed, thus causing large-
scale impacts.

Remarks: Mineral extraction should be carefully examined
through contact with local mineral professionals, private
industries and professional societies.

Data Sources:

Voorhees (1975).

References:

Environmental Protection Agency (1973)

ACCOUNT: ENVIRONMENTAL QUALITY

CATEGORY: TERRESTRIAL

SUBCATEGORY: CRITICAL COMMUNITY RELATIONSHIPS

VARIABLE: SPECIES DIVERSITY

Definition and Measurement of Baseline Conditions: Species
diversity is a measured parameter which may be used as an
indicator of the richness of a community or geographical area
in species.   In its simplest level of examination, species
diversity corresponds to the number of species present (Collier,
et al, 1973).   Since the relative abundance of a species is
important to the function of a community, often measures of
diversity also account for the equitability of abundance or
importance of the various species.
   Measurement involves consideration of the numbers of species as well as the numbers of individuals within each species.

Prediction of Impacts: The diversity measure used is based on
the logarithm of the density of the individuals of the dominant terrestrial plant species.   These plants are used as indicators of overall terrestrial diversity.   Data on species
and density of the dominant plant species are collected from
the different habitats in the terrestrial ecosystems within
the project boundaries.   The log of the number of individuals
(y-axis) is plotted against the number of species (x-axis)
and a regression line is fitted to the data for each habitat.
The number of species per 1000 individuals is taken from each
regression line.   The mean number of species per 1000 individuals for all habitats sampled is the value of the parameter "with" or "without" the project:

$$\text{Parameter Estimate} = \frac{\text{Mean Number of Species}}{1000 \text{ Individuals}}$$

<u>Functional Curve</u> (Battelle Environmental Evaluation System, 1972)

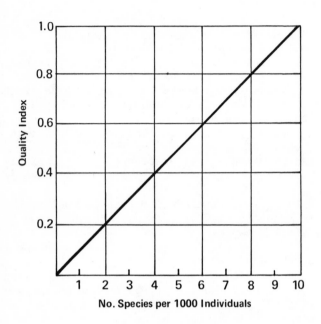

Remarks: Species diversity tends to be low in physically controlled systems and high in biologically controlled systems (Odum, 1971).

Data Sources:

      Battelle Environmental Evaluation System (1972).
      Collier, et al (1973).
      Odum (1971).

References:

      Patton (1975).
      Peet (1974).

AQUATIC VARIABLES

ACCOUNT: ENVIRONMENTAL QUALITY

CATEGORY: AQUATIC

SUBCATEGORY: POPULATIONS

VARIABLE: NATURAL VEGETATION

Definition and Measurement of Baseline Conditions: A population is defined as a group of organisms consisting of the same
species. Natural aquatic vegetation may be either attached
vascular plants or unattached, floating plant species. Aquatic
vegetation contributes significantly to total production in
aquatic systems, and provides desirable habitat and food resources for inhabiting heterotrophs.

The magnitude modified by quality approach is used in
measuring the variable. The magnitude is the surface area
of water and the modifier is an estimate of the quality of
that water. Four basic aquatic habitats are recognized:
(1) streams and rivers, (2) lakes, ponds, and impoundments,
(3) wetlands, including swamps and marshes, and (4) estuarine
and marine (Battelle Environmental Evaluation System, 1972).

Prediction of Impacts: The quality of the area in streams or
lakes is estimated on a 0 to 1 scale with five qualities recognized (Table 1). A stream or lake should meet most but not
necessarily all the standards included in the description in
order to be assigned to a particular quality level. For this
parameter, the plant productivity is particularly important
in assigning areas to a quality level. Wetland quality is
classified into three levels (Table 2).

The surface acreage in each quality classification is
determined and multiplied by the corresponding weight to give
a weighted acreage. The sum of the weighted acreages divided
by the total aquatic surface acreage and multiplied by 100 is
the percent value of the parameter "with" and "without" the
project:

$$\text{Parameter Estimate} = \sum_{I}^{N} \frac{\text{Surface Acreage x K}}{\text{Total Water Surface Area}} \text{ X } 100$$

where

    N = number of quality areas
    K = water quality classification

Changes in water surface area caused by the project should
appear both in the areas of each quality type and in the total
water surface area.

TABLE 1: THE QUALITY CATEGORIES USED FOR LAKES, STREAMS
AND ESTUARIES AND THEIR WEIGHTS

Quality Category	Description	Weight
A	High plant productivity, good water quality, good year-round water supply, diverse food web, large fish population	1.0
B	Moderate-to-high plant productivity, good water quality, some water level fluctuation, diverse food web, moderate-to-large fish population	0.75
C	Moderate plant productivity, fair water quality, water level fluctuation, simplified food web, moderate fish population	0.50
D	Low plant productivity, poor water quality, water level fluctuation, simplified food web, small fish population	0.25
E	Very low to zero plant productivity, poor water quality, intermittent water supply, highly simplified food web, no fish population	0

TABLE 2: THE QUALITY CATEGORIES USED FOR WETLANDS
AND THEIR WEIGHTS

Quality Category	Description	Weight
A	High plant productivity, good water supply, year-round waterfowl usage, good waterfowl production, good hunting, good migrant bird usage	1.0
B	Moderate plant productivity, fluctuating water supply, some year-round waterfowl usage, limited waterfowl production, limited hunting, good migrant bird usage	0.67
C	Low plant productivity, intermittent water supply, limited waterfowl usage, no waterfowl production, poor hunting, limited migrant bird usage	0.33

Functional Curve

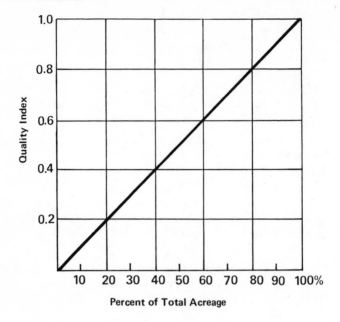

Percent of Total Acreage

Remarks: High plant productivity may be common in eutrophic, nutrient-rich water and therefore be characterized by poor water quality.

Data Sources:

   Battelle Environmental Evaluation System (1972).

References:

   Poole (1974).

60

ACCOUNT: ENVIRONMENTAL QUALITY

CATEGORY: AQUATIC

SUBCATEGORY: POPULATIONS

VARIABLE: WETLAND VEGETATION

Definition and Measurement of Baseline Conditions: Wetland vegetation includes all rooted emergent vegetation, with particular emphasis on swamp and marsh vegetation. This vegetation is an important environmental indicator of production because it is a relatively efficient converter of radiant energy into chemical energy. The principal way to measure changes in wetland vegetation would be to measure changes in productivity. Productivity is defined as the rate of storage of organic matter in plant tissues in excess of the respiratory utilization of the plants during the period of measurement.

Vegetation samples (based upon some experimental design) are taken throughout the growing season. Samples are weighed and the caloric content of the vegetation established. Production is expressed as lb/acre or some other appropriate measure. Seasonal and yearly cycles of productivity can then be followed.

Prediction of Impacts: Estimates of impact under various project alternatives can be calculated using habitat area and productivity as follows:

$$\text{Variable Estimate} = \sum_{I}^{N} (\text{Habitat acreage} \times \text{productivity})$$

where

N = Number of habitat types within project area.

Since wetland vegetation areas are so important in providing nutrients to entire ecosystems and habitat for many aquatic species during at least some stage in their life cycle, changes in acreage or productivity should be carefully evaluated. A decrease in acreage would result not only in a drop in productivity but in a loss of nutrients utilized by phytoplankton in the adjacent aquatic areas. This could result in significant impact on the aquatic ecosystem. Similarly, a decrease in acreage would result in the loss of food to those herbivores living on the marshes or the detritus feeders in the aquatic ecosystem (Battelle Dredging Impact Assessment Method, 1974).

Functional Curve:

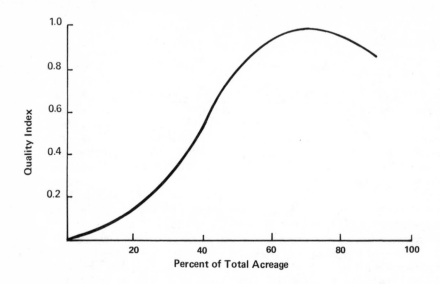

Remarks: A decrease in wetland plant acreage could allow greater nutrient inflow to adjacent lakes.

Data Sources:

Battelle Dredging Impact Assessment Method (1974).

References:

Singh, Lauenroth and Steinhurst (1975).
Teal and Kanwisher (1970).

ACCOUNT: ENVIRONMENTAL QUALITY

CATEGORY: AQUATIC

SUBCATEGORY: POPULATIONS

VARIABLE: ZOOPLANKTON

Definition and Measurement of Baseline Conditions: Zooplankton include small animals of weak swimming ability or without swimming ability that are free floating or drifting biota. Two types of zooplankters must be considered. The first type, the holoplankter, includes forms like the copepods which spend their entire life cycle as plankton. The second type, the meroplankton, include such things as the larval stages of invertebrates and the eggs and larvae of most fish species. The zooplankton have their importance in the aquatic food web by being an initial consumer of energy fixed by the phytoplankton, and by themselves providing a link between primary production and higher trophic levels. Measurements of species richness (R), species composition, and species diversity (d) indices should be conducted to evaluate the contribution of this trophic level to production and ecosystem stability. Because of their role as primary consumers in aquatic ecosystems, the effect of zooplankton fluctuations on higher trophic levels should be considered.

Prediction of Impacts: Capabilities for predicting zooplankton populations are generally not well established; however, the model of Patten et al. (1975), which utilizes the relationships between phytoplankton and zooplankton should be consulted.

Functional Curves:

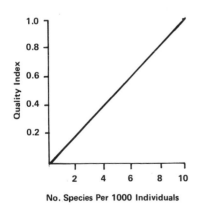

No. Species Per 1000 Individuals

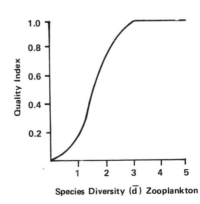

Species Diversity (d̄) Zooplankton

63

Remarks: In assessing zooplankton populations, turnover rates together and temporary (seasonal) occurances of planktivorous species need to be considered.

Data Sources:

Patten (1975).

References:

Battelle Dredging Impact Assessment Method (1974).

ACCOUNT: ENVIRONMENTAL QUALITY

CATEGORY: AQUATIC

SUBCATEGORY: POPULATIONS

VARIABLE: PHYTOPLANKTON

Definition and Measurement of Baseline Conditions: Phytoplankton include all drifting or floating aquatic plants.
Usually, these plants are single celled and autotrophic.
Phytoplankton, as primary producers, contribute appreciably
to total production within aquatic systems.
　　The most popular method of assessing the growth of phytoplankton populations, apart from direct counts of individuals
of various species making up the phytoplankton community,
is through the determination of primary productivity, or
photosynthetic activity, which is the rate at which CO_2 is
converted to organic matter. In evaluating the significance
of phytoplankton changes associated with any planning alternative, changes in the primary productivity of the impact area
should be considered (Battelle Dredging Impact Assessment
Method, 1974).

Prediction of Impacts: Phytoplankton are at the base of the
food pyramid. Decreases in abundance of phytoplankton, as
indicated by a decrease in primary productivity, may effect
adversely zooplankton populations. Since zooplankton form a
significant food resource for most juvenile fish and the
adults of some important species (e.g., the herring family),
a decrease in phytoplankton abundance may eventually have
adverse effects upon higher trophic levels.

Functional Curves:

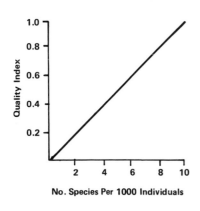

No. Species Per 1000 Individuals

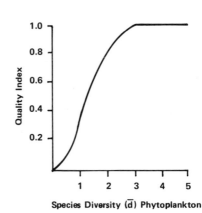

Species Diversity (d̄) Phytoplankton

65

Remarks: Fluctuations in phytoplankton growth and density occur seasonally and are time related. Also since plankti- vorous species are seasonal in occurence, phytoplankton densi- ties can be expected to vary in accordance with the abundance to planktivores. Productivity may be decreased without a decrease in planktonic organisms, since zooplankton are not dependent totally upon phytoplankton production.

Data Sources:

Battelle Dredging Impact Assessment Method (1974).

References:

Wetzel (1975).

ACCOUNT: ENVIRONMENTAL QUALITY

CATEGORY: AQUATIC

SUBCATEGORY: POPULATIONS

VARIABLE: SPORT FISH

Definition and Measurement of Baseline Conditions: Sport
fish refers to those species of fish which are pursued with
various techniques by anglers either for the fish's gamy
qualities or as a food fish. This group includes certain
species of the families Ictaluridae, Centrarchidae and Per-
cichthyidae. Sport fish are an important resource to fisher-
man and a useful indicator of production.

Measurement is accomplished via the concept of an area
times a quality modifier. As shown in Table 1, quality is
divided into the same five levels as for the aquatic natural
vegetation. In assigning areas to a quality level all the
standards describing a particular level should be considered,
but the size of the sport fish population is the most important. Weighted acreages are obtained by multiplying the
area assigned to a quality level by the weight of that level.
The sum of the weighted acreages divided by the total water
surface area and multiplied by 100 is the parameter value
(Battelle Environmental Evaluation System, 1972):

Prediction of Impacts: Estimates of impact under various
project alternatives can be calculated using quality categories as indicated.

$$\text{Parameter Estimate} = \sum_{I}^{N} \frac{(\text{Surface Area} \times K)}{\text{Total Water Surface Area}} \times 100$$

where

N = number of quality areas
K = quality classification weight

Changes in water surface area caused by the project
should appear in both the appropriate weighted acreages and
in the total water surface area.

TABLE 1: THE QUALITY CATEGORIES USED FOR LAKES, STREAMS,
AND ESTUARIES AND THEIR WEIGHTS

Quality Category	Description	Weight
A	High plant productivity, good water quality, good year-round water supply, diverse food web, large fish population	1.0
B	Moderate-to-high plant productivity, good water quality, some water level fluctuation, diverse food web, moderate-to-large fish population	0.75
C	Moderate plant productivity, fair water quality, water level fluctuation, simplified food web, moderate fish population	0.50
D	Low plant productivity, poor water quality, water level fluctuation, simplified food web, small fish population	0.25
E	Very low to zero plant productivity, poor water quality, intermittent water supply, highly simplified food web, no fish population	0

Functional Curve

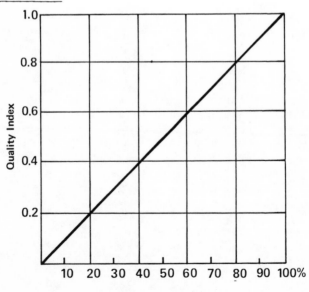

Percent of Total Acreage

68

Remarks: Another excellent modifier that may be used is based on the annual sport fish production in pounds per acre or pounds per stream or river mile. The range of production data for an area could be weighted on a 0 to 1 scale as done for the quality modifier now used for this parameter. Currently, data on sport fish production in pounds per acre or mile is available from most State Fish and Game Departments.

Data Sources:

Battelle Environmental Evaluation System (1972).

References:

Jenkins and Morais (1971).

ACCOUNT: ENVIRONMENTAL QUALITY

CATEGORY: AQUATIC

SUBCATEGORY: POPULATIONS

VARIABLE: COMMERCIAL FISHERIES

Definition and Measurement of Baseline Conditions: Commercial
fisheries pertain to those aquatic organisms that can be obtained in quantities for commerce. Such organisms are composed primarily of species of fish, including members of the
familiar Clupudae, Cyprinidae, Catastomidae, Atherinidae and
Mugilidae; although in the marine commercial fisheries, many
organisms other than fish enter the catch, e.g., shellfish
including both crustaceans and mollusks.
    Measurement is accomplished by determining area and
multiplying by a quality modifier. A linear relationship
exists between the weighted percent of the area available to
commercial fisheries and the environmental quality. The
magnitude is the area, and the maximum possible commercial
habitat in surface acres of water within the project boundaries is 100 percent. The actual area inhabited modified by
an estimate of quality is the value of the parameter "with"
or "without" the project. (Battelle Environmental Evaluation
System, 1972).

Prediction of Impacts: The quality modifier, because of man's
interest, is based on the dollar value of the annual commercial catch. The dollar values are weighted on a 0 to 1 scale:

$$
\begin{array}{rcl}
1.00 & --- & \$1,000,000 \\
0.67 & --- & 100,000 \\
0.33 & --- & 10,000 \\
0 & --- & 1,000
\end{array}
$$

The economic threshold for commercial fisheries is about
$1,000. For dollar values intermediate between two levels,
interpolation is necessary to determine the exact value of
the modifier. (Note the logarithmic nature of the weighting.)
The modifier times the inhabited area is the weighted area
"with" or "without" the project. This product divided by
the total available area is the parameter estimate used in
the functional curve:

$$\text{Parameter Estimate} = \frac{\text{Area Inhabited} \times K}{\text{Maximum Habitat Area}} \times 100,$$

where

    K = Weighted dollar value

70

Functional Curve

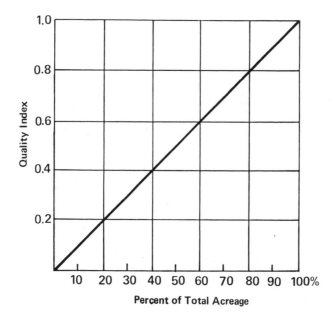

Percent of Total Acreage

Remarks: This evaluation assumes a homogenous area, i.e.,
no differentiation between near-shore and blue-water species
is made, although this relationship should be considered.

Data Sources:

   Battelle Environmental Evaluation System (1972).

References:

   Jenkins (1968).
   Ricker (1968).

ACCOUNT: ENVIRONMENTAL QUALITY

CATEGORY: AQUATIC

SUBCATEGORY: POPULATIONS

VARIABLE: INTERTIDAL ORGANISMS

Definition and Measurement of Baseline Conditions: This group
contains all the organisms, both plant and animal, which
inhabit the zone between the high and the low tides in those
areas where there is a noticeable tide effect. Many of the
species found in the intertidal zone are also found in the
benthic and epibenthic areas; however, because of the unique
environmental stresses imposed on inhabitants of the intertidal zone, they are being included here as a separate group.
     The intertidal zone biota can include both primary
producers (macroalgae) and primary consumers (barnacles,
clams, mussels, etc.). Under comparable conditions, macro-
phytic communities are more productive per unit area than
phytoplankton communities. In some areas the intertidal
fauna include commercial species like the soft clam, Mya
arenaria. The variety of organisms included in the intertidal zone community make that community an excellent indicator of water quality. Species composition and population
levels can be determined from samples taken directly from
the intertidal zone.

Prediction of Impacts: There is no well-established technique
for predicting fluctuations in intertidal communities, although the study by Dayton (1975) should be consulted because
of the inherent diversity in the intertidal communities, a
decrease in diversity is often quickly obvious, and may be
attributable to a decrease in water quality. Excess siltation
during the period when the larvae of intertidal invertebrates
or the zoopores of intertidal macrophytes are in the water
column and preparing to set could cover potential setting
spaces, thereby decreasing additions to the community. Decrease in dissolved oxygen or increase in toxic material
could have adverse effects upon the existing biota.

Functional Curve:

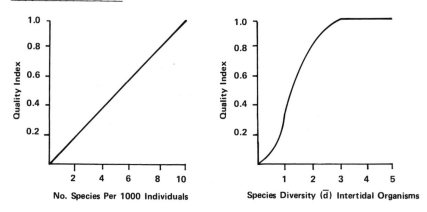

No. Species Per 1000 Individuals

Species Diversity (d̄) Intertidal Organisms

Remarks: Intertidal communities are sensitive to environmental change, as they appear to be influenced appreciably by ambient conditions and also to adjacent terrestrial conditions.

Data Sources:

Dayton (1975).

References:

Battelle Dredging Impact Assessment Method (1974).

ACCOUNT: ENVIRONMENTAL QUALITY

CATEGORY: AQUATIC

SUBCATEGORY: POPULATIONS

VARIABLE: BENTHOS/EPIBENTHOS

Definition and Measurement of Baseline Conditions: This
variable includes those animals which live on or in the
bottom of all types of waterbodies (streams, lakes, rivers,
estuaries, bays, etc.). Many of these benthic and epibenthic animals are commercially valuable. They include the
various hard- and soft-shell clams, oysters, scallops,
lobsters, crabs, and some of the non-commercial species, like
worms and smaller bivalve vertebrates. Impacts on the
benthos/epibenthos can be measured directly by changes in
the numbers of a given species or by changes in the numbers
of species. (Battelle Dredging Impact Assessment Method,
1974).

Prediction of Impacts: The value function and the techniques
for evaluating aquatic species diversity are similar to the
rationale employed toward Critical Community Relationships,
except benthos is used as the indicator group. A variety
of aquatic habitats are sampled and the mean numbers of
species per 1000 individuals is used as the parameter value.
Changes resulting from the proposed project may be predicted
by measuring their parameter in similar habitats where
projects are completed and operating.

Functional Curve:

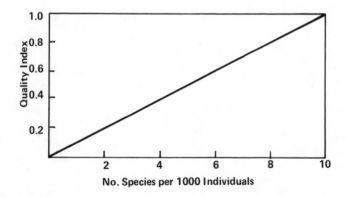

No. Species per 1000 Individuals

Remarks: Field sampling and monitoring programs of benthos
populations should encompass seasonal changes which can be
expected to occur naturally within the region.

74

Data Sources:

Battelle Dredging Impact Assessment Method (1974).

References:

Poole (1974).

ACCOUNT: ENVIRONMENTAL QUALITY

CATEGORY: AQUATIC

SUBCATEGORY: POPULATIONS

VARIABLE: WATERFOWL

Definition and Measurement of Baseline Conditions: Waterfowl
is defined as those species of birds which frequent aquatic
environments and utilize such habitats as feeding and breeding sites. Collectively, this group is composed of swimming
game birds as distinguished from upland game birds and shore
birds. Waterfowl utilization of wetland habitats relates to
the suitability of such aquatic environments in providing
resting, feeding and breeding sites for waterfowl.
      Waterfowl magnitude is measured as the area of waterfowl
habitat within the project boundaries, while the modifier is
an estimate of the quality of that habitat in reference to
waterfowl use. The total area of wetland habitat is equated
with 100 percent. The quality of these wetland habitats is
weighted on a 0 to 1 basis using the three categories (Table 1).
The area of each of the three qualities of habitats is determined and multiplied by the corresponding modifier. Resulting weighted acreages are summed and divided by the total
wetland area to give the value for the parameter "without" the
project (Battelle Environmental Evaluation System, 1972).

$$\text{Parameter Estimate} = \sum_{I}^{N} \frac{\text{(Wetland Habitat Area x K)}}{\text{Total Wetland Area}} \text{ x } 100$$

where

        N = number of habitats
        K = quality modifier weight

Prediction of Impacts: Predicted changes in the quality and
acreage of wetland habitats and in the total wetland acreage
are used as above to calculate the parameter value "with"
project.

TABLE 1:   THE QUALITY CATEGORIES USED FOR WETLANDS
            AND THEIR WEIGHTS

Quality Category	Description	Weight
A	High plant productivity, good water supply, year-round waterfowl usage, good waterfowl production, good hunting, good migrant bird usage	1.0
B	Moderate plant productivity, fluctuating water supply, some year-round waterfowl usage, limited waterfowl production, limited hunting, good migrant bird usage	0.67
C	Low plant productivity, intermittent water supply, limited waterfowl usage, no waterfowl production, poor hunting, limited migrant bird usage	0.33

Functional Curve:

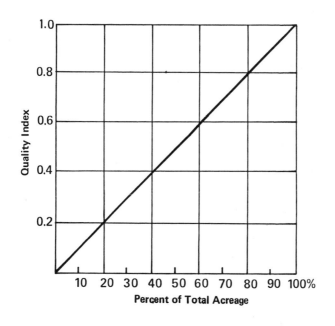

Remarks: A second modifier in addition to wetland habitat quality, is the waterfowl-day use of the wetlands. Waterfowl-day use would be weighted in the same manner as wetland quality with the categories being low, moderate, and high use in order of increasing weight. This modifier would provide a better estimate of the importance of the wetland habitats than would hunter success or other such measures because it would include all waterfowl - migrants, residents, game, and others. Data on waterfowl-day use can be obtained from the Fish and Wildlife Service or State Departments of Wildlife Conservation.

Data Sources:

Battelle Environmental Evaluation System (1972).

References:

Battelle Dredging Impact Assessment Method (1974).

ACCOUNT: ENVIRONMENTAL QUALITY

CATEGORY: AQUATIC

SUBCATEGORY: HABITATS

VARIABLE: STREAM

Definition and Measurement of Baseline Conditions: An inland
body of water which characteristically flows or moves as
distinguished from standing bodies of water.   Streams are
considered from the standpoint of serving as plant and animal
habitat.   Evaluation of this habitat type is based on the
composite of eight key parameters.   (Lower Mississippi Valley
Division, 1976).   These parameters were identified in a joint
study effort between biologists at the Lower Mississippi
Valley Division and WES.   Approximately 20 persons participated
in the study.   Key outputs from the study were: (1) the
identification of parameters associated with three terrestrial
habitat types (bottomland forest, upland forest, and open
lands) and four aquatic habitat types (stream, freshwater
lake, river swamp, and non-river swamp); (2) the assignment
of relative importance weights to the identified parameters
for each habitat type; and (3) the presentation of functional
curves for each identified parameter.   Evaluation of field
applications of the outputs is under current study.

The eight parameters for a stream habitat are:

1.   Sinuosity -- an indicator of the diversity of
     habitats within a stream reach, expressed as
     the ratio of stream length to straight line
     distance.

2.   Dominant centrarchids -- species composition of
     major predator/sport fish family i.e., (Centrarchidae)
     which includes largemouth, smallmouth, and
     spotted bass; black and white crappie; and a
     variety of sunfish species.

3.   Mean low water width -- average stream width
     during low water season.

4.   Turbidity -- a measure of the reduction of
     light penetration into the water due largely
     to the presence of suspended material and
     thus an indication of the degree of aquatic
     photosynthetic activity reduction.

79

5. Total dissolved solids -- an indicator of potential productivity expressed as the residue upon evaporation at 180° C in ppm (weighted mean).

6. Chemical type -- an indicator of potential productivity noted as the prevalent chemical type of inflowing water.

   Key: (1) Ca-Mg, CO_3-HCO_3 (3) Na-K, CO_3-HCO_3

   (2) Ca-Mg, SO_4-Cl   (4) Na-K, SO_4-Cl

7. Diversity of fishes -- the species diversity index, d, is a measure of community structure and an indication of ecological stability expressed by the following function:

$$d = - \sum_{1}^{s} \frac{n_i}{n} (\log_2 \frac{n_i}{n})$$

   where

   s = numbers of species.
   n = numbers of individuals, and
   n_i= numbers of individuals per species.

8. Diversity of benthos -- see 7 above.

Prediction of Impacts: See discussion for Bottomland Forest for Terrestrial/Habitats/Land Use. The importance weights for the eight parameters for streams are:

PARAMETER	WEIGHT
1. Sinuosity	12
2. Dominant Centrarchid	13
3. Mean Low Water Width	7
4. Turbidity	13
5. TDS	10
6. Chemical Type	10
7. Diversity of Fishes	15
8. Diversity of Benthos	20

Functional Curves: See the following 8 curves.

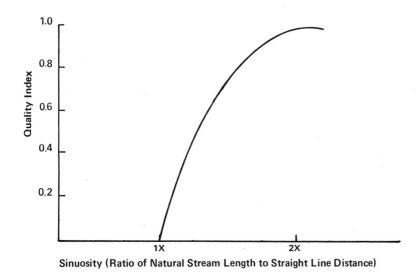

Sinuosity (Ratio of Natural Stream Length to Straight Line Distance)

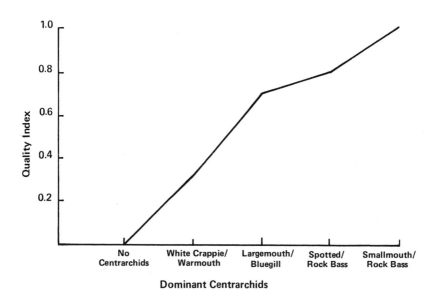

Dominant Centrarchids

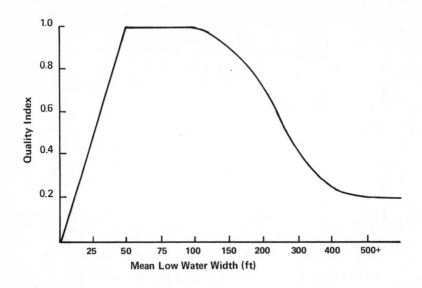

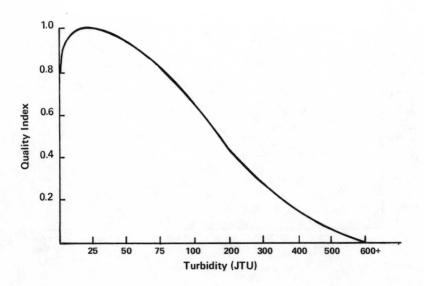

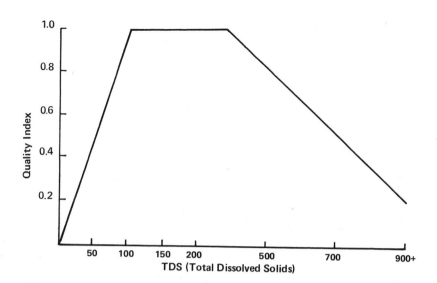

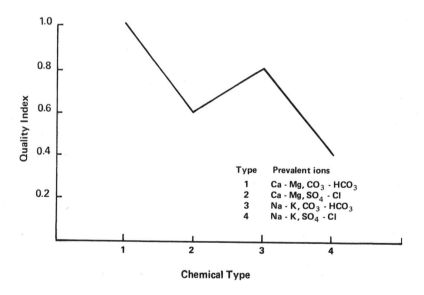

Type	Prevalent ions
1	Ca - Mg, CO_3 - HCO_3
2	Ca - Mg, SO_4 - Cl
3	Na - K, CO_3 - HCO_3
4	Na - K, SO_4 - Cl

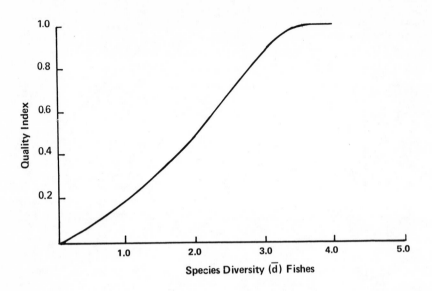

Species Diversity ($\overline{d}$) Fishes

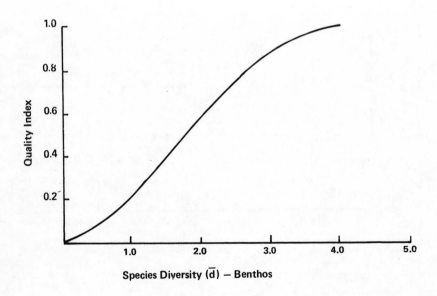

Species Diversity ($\overline{d}$) — Benthos

Remarks: The environmental characteristics of streams vary appreciably among geographical regions due to ambient conditions and soil characteristics. Streams of western states can be expected to possess, under natural influences, significantly different characteristics herein defined as components of or high environmental quality.

Data Sources:

Lower Mississippi Valley Division (1976).

References:

Bechtel and Copeland (1970).
Hynes (1970).

ACCOUNT: ENVIRONMENTAL QUALITY

CATEGORY: AQUATIC

SUBCATEGORY: HABITATS

VARIABLE: FRESHWATER LAKE

Definition and Measurement of Baseline Conditions: An inland body of standing water of relatively large size (>500 surface acres), which provides plant and animal habitat.

Evaluation of this habitat type is based on the composite of ten key parameters (Lower Mississippi Valley Division, 1976).   These parameters were identified in a joint study effort between biologists at the Lower Mississippi Valley Division and WES.   Approximately 20 persons participated in the study.   Key outputs from the study were: (1) the identification of parameters associated with three terrestrial habitat types (bottomland forest, upland forest, and open lands) and four aquatic habitat types (stream, freshwater lake, river swamp, and non-river swamp); (2) the assignment of relative importance weights to the identified parameters for each habitat type; and (3) the presentation of functional curves for each identified parameter.   Evaluation of field applications of the outputs is under current study.

The ten parameters for a freshwater lake habitat are:

1.   Mean depth -- expressed in feet at normal pool elevation.

2.   Turbidity -- see discussion under Stream variables.

3.   Total dissolved solids -- see discussion under Stream variables.

4.   Chemical type -- see discussion under Stream variables.

5.   Shore development -- the ratio of shoreline length to the circumference of a circle equal to that of the lake.

$$\text{Shore development} = \frac{S}{2\sqrt{a}}$$

where S = length of shoreline, and a = area

6.   Spring flooding above vegetation line -- a significant factor contributing to the establishment of strong year class production of sport fish, primarily largemouth bass. Expressed as the percent of normal pool area flooded times the number of days flooded.

86

For example, flooding of a river lake causing a doubling of surface acreage for a four-month period would be 100 percent times 120 days = 12,000 units which would yield a curve score of approximately 0.95.

7. Standing crop of fishes -- estimated total standing crop of fish in pounds per acre derived from recovery following rotenone treatment.

8. Standing crop of sport fish -- estimated standing crop of fish species generally considered game species expressed in pounds per acre.

9. Diversity of fishes -- see discussion under Stream variables.

10. Diversity of benthos -- see discussion under Stream variables.

Prediction of Impacts: Review discussion of Bottomland Forest for Terrestrial/Habitats/Land Use. The importance weights for the ten parameters for lakes are:

PARAMETER	WEIGHT
1. Mean Depth	7
2. Turbidity	10
3. TDS	7
4. Chemical Type	7
5. Shore Development	10
6. Spring Flooding	11
7. Standing Crop of Fishes	9
8. Standing Crop of Sport Fishes	13
9. Diversity of Fishes	14
10. Diversity of Benthos	12

Functional Curves: See the following 10 curves.

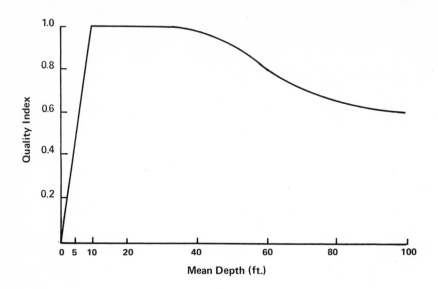

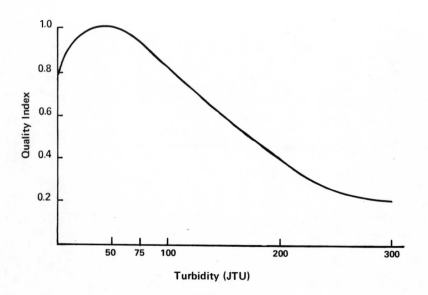

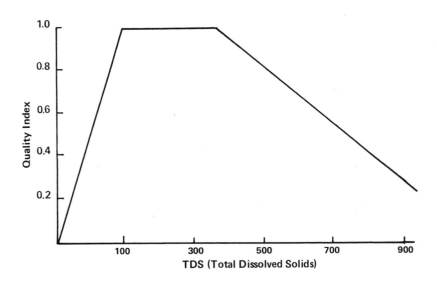

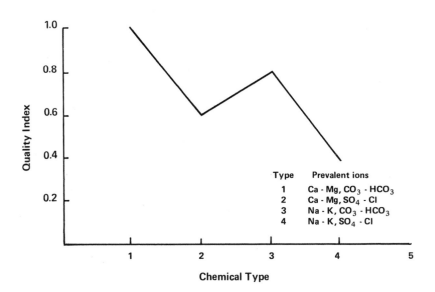

89

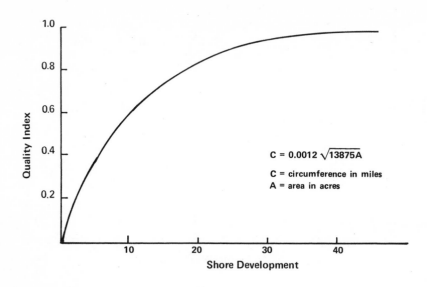

$C = 0.0012 \sqrt{13875A}$

C = circumference in miles
A = area in acres

Shore Development

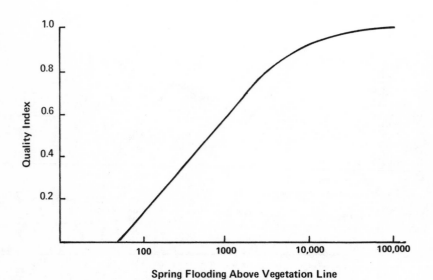

Spring Flooding Above Vegetation Line
(as percent of normal pool area X days flooded)

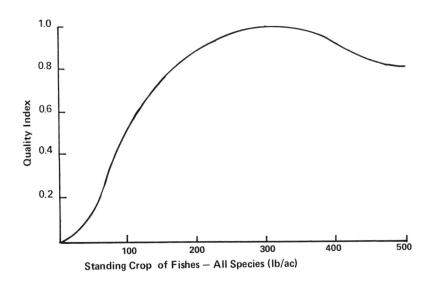

Standing Crop of Fishes — All Species (lb/ac)

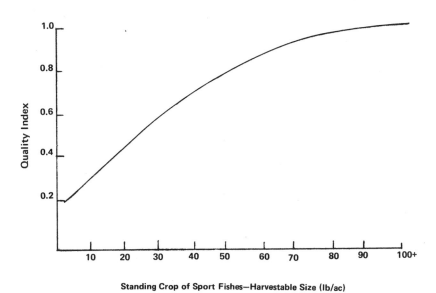

Standing Crop of Sport Fishes—Harvestable Size (lb/ac)

91

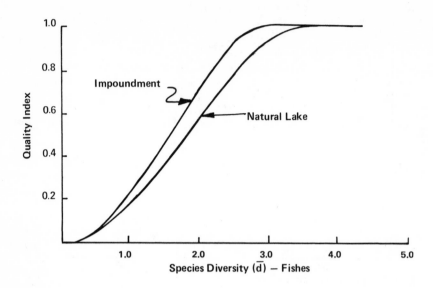

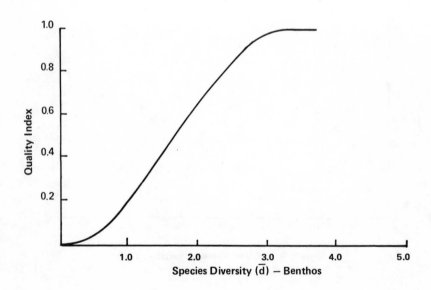

Remarks: Due to the inherent characteristics of different geographical regions, the environmental features of lakes can be expected to differ significantly. Thus, the features of high environmental quality in lakes, under natural conditions, cannot be expected to be commensurate.

Data Sources:

Lower Mississippi Valley Division (1976).

References:

Jenkins (1968).
Ransom and Dorris (1972).

ACCOUNT: ENVIRONMENTAL QUALITY

CATEGORY: AQUATIC

SUBCATEGORY: HABITATS

VARIABLE: RIVER SWAMP

Definition and Measurement of Baseline Conditions: A river
swamp is a lowland area within the floodplain receiving considerable in- and out-flow of water via means of river discharge.   Such areas are normally flooded only during periods
of high-water discharge from a river.   Evaluation of this
habitat type is based on the composite of six key parameters
(Lower Mississippi Valley Division, 1976).   These parameters
were identified in a joint study effort between biologists
at the Lower Mississippi Valley Division and WES.   Approximately 20 persons participated in this study.   Key outputs
from the study were: (1) the identification of parameters
associated with three terrestrial habitat types (bottomland
forest, upland forest, and open lands) and four aquatic habitat
types (stream, freshwater lake, river swamp, and non-river
swamp); (2) the assignment of relative importance weights to
the identified parameters for each habitat type; and (3) the
presentation of functional curves for each identified parameter.   Evaluation of field applications of the outputs is
under current study.

    The six parameters for a river swamp habitat are:

1. Species associations -- dominant species
    composition.

2. Percent forest cover -- percentage of the
    habitat covered by tree canopy.

3. Percent flooded annually -- percentage of
    habitat area which experiences annual
    flooding.

4. Groundcover diversity -- the average number
    of groundcover species present within the
    sample area.

5. Percent coverage by groundcover -- average
    percentage of habitat area covered by
    groundcover species.

6. Days subject to river overflow -- estimated
    number of days during which a significant
    proportion of the habitat area is flooded
    annually.

Prediction of Impacts: Review discussion for Bottomland
Forest for Terrestrial/Habitats/Land Use. The importance
weights for the six parameters for freshwater river swamps
are:

PARAMETERS	WEIGHT
1. Species Associations	22
2. Percent Forest Cover	17
3. Percent Flooded Annually	18
4. Groundcover Diversity	12
5. Percent Coverage by Groundwater	13
6. Days Subject to River Overflow	18

Functional Curves: See the following six curves.

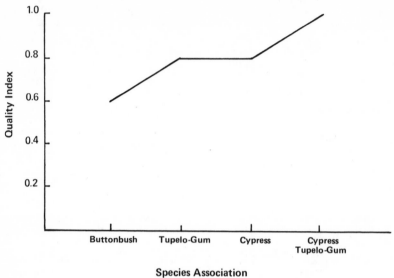

Species Association

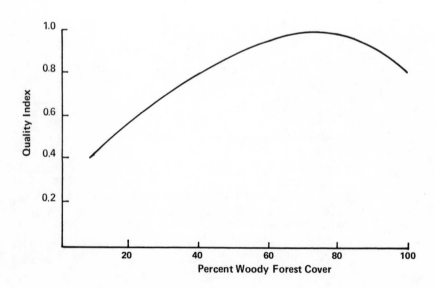

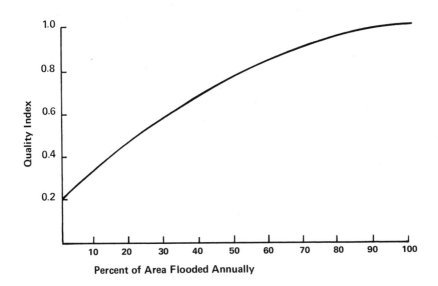

Percent of Area Flooded Annually

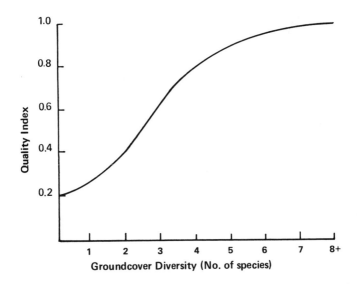

Groundcover Diversity (No. of species)

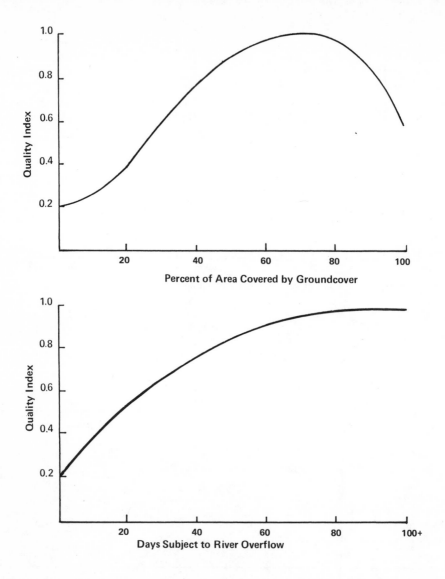

Remarks: Environmental parameters evaluated for this variable are regionally specific and can be expected to differ geographically.

Data Sources:

    Lower Mississippi Valley Division (1976).

References:

    Yeager (1949).
    Wharton (1970).

ACCOUNT: ENVIRONMENTAL QUALITY

CATEGORY: AQUATIC

SUBCATEGORY: HABITATS

VARIABLE: NON-RIVER SWAMP

Definition and Measurement of Baseline Conditions: A non-
river swamp is a lowland area which does not receive periodic
flooding from a river, but receives water primarily from
underground seepage, runoff, or springs. Evaluation of this
habitat type is based on the composite of five key parameters
(Lower Mississippi Valley Division, 1976). These parameters
were identified in a joint study effort between biologists at
the Lower Mississippi Valley Division and WES. Approximately
20 persons participated in the study. Key outputs from the
study were: (1) the identification of parameters associated
with three terrestrial habitat types (bottomland forest,
upland forest, and open lands) and four aquatic habitat types
(stream, freshwater lake, river swamp, and non-river swamp);
(2) the assignment of relative importance weights to the
identified parameters for each habitat type; and (3) the presentation of functional curves for each identified parameter.
Evaluation of field applications of the outputs is under current study.
    The five key parameters for a non-river swamp habitat
are as follows: species associations, percent forest cover,
percent flooded annually, groundcover diversity, and percent
coverage by groundcover. For definitions of these parameters
see River Swamp variable (Lower Mississippi Valley Division,
1976).

Prediction of Impacts: Review discussion for Bottomland
Forest for Terrestrial/Habitats/Land Use category. The
importance weights for the five parameters for freshwater
non-river swamps are:

PARAMETER	WEIGHT
1. Species Associations	28
2. Percent Forest Cover	21
3. Percent Flooded Annually	23
4. Groundcover Diversity	14
5. Percent Coverage by Groundcover	14

Functional Curves: See the following 5 curves.

99

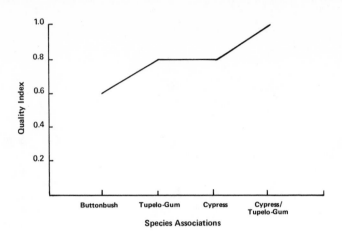

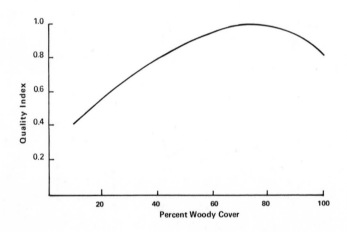

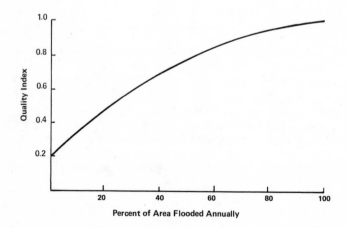

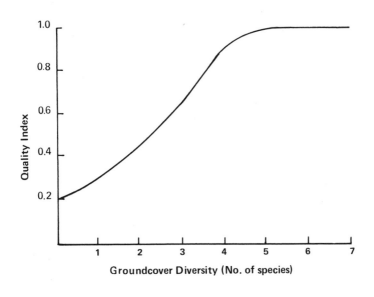

Groundcover Diversity (No. of species)

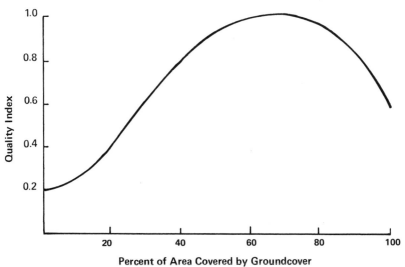

Percent of Area Covered by Groundcover

Remarks: Assessment of environmental quality for this variable does not include herbacious flora composition.

Data Sources:

Lower Mississippi Valley Division (1976).

References:

Yeager (1949).

ACCOUNT: ENVIRONMENTAL QUALITY

CATEGORY: AQUATIC

SUBCATEGORY: WATER QUALITY

VARIABLE: pH

Definition and Measurement of Baseline Conditions: The pH of
a solution refers to its hydrogen ion activity and is expressed
as the logarithm of the reciprocal of the hydrogen ion activity
in moles per liter at a given temperature. The term pH is
used widely to express the intensity of the acid or alkaline
condition of a solution. When pH is between 0 and 7, this is
referred to as the acid range, and when pH is between 7 and 14,
this reflects the alkaline range. The pH of most surface
waters will range between 6.5 and 9.0.
    The existing water quality in terms of pH should be des-
cribed for the project area. Particular attention should be
given to possible natural or man-made seasonal variations in
pH.

Prediction of Impacts: Prediction of the impacts of a potential project should include consideration of the extent of
departure of pH from the normal (natural) values in an area.
The functional curve shown below is based on the concept that
a decrease in environmental quality occurs when the pH in a
given local is changed from its normal (natural) value. Attention should be addressed to potential changes in pH that might
result from project construction and operation. If the project
involves water impoundment, there is considerable literature
which describes anticipated pH changes. If industrial development is anticipated, then consideration would need to be given
to the potential pH changes resulting from industrial discharges.

Functional Curve (Battelle Environmental Evaluation System, 1972):

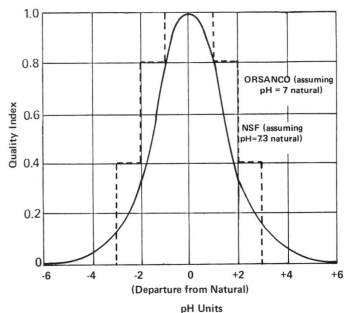

ORSANCO = Ohio River Sanitation Commission
NSF = National Sanitation Foundation

Remarks: Careful consideration needs to be given to establishing the "natural" pH for the project area.

Data Sources:

Battelle Environmental Evaluation System (1972).

References:

Sawyer and McCarty (1967).

ACCOUNT: ENVIRONMENTAL QUALITY

CATEGORY: AQUATIC

SUBCATEGORY: WATER QUALITY

VARIABLE: TURBIDITY

Definition and Measurement of Baseline Conditions: Turbidity
is a measure of the extent to which light passing through water
is reduced by scattering induced by suspended and colloidal
material.   The unit of expression is the Jackson Turbidity Unit,
where 1 JTU is equal to the turbidity caused by 1 mg/l of SiO_2
in water.   In lake or other waters existing under relatively
quiescent conditions, most of the turbidity will be due to
colloidal and extremely fine dispersions.   In rivers under
flood conditions, turbidity will be primarily comprised of
relatively coarse dispersions.   Turbidity is of concern in
surface water courses due to esthetic considerations, filter-
ability, and disinfection.   In general, as turbidity levels
increase esthetic value decreases, the filtration of water is
rendered more difficult and costly, and the effectiveness of
disinfection procedures is reduced.   Turbidity in water may
result from naturally occurring materials, or from man-related
activities such as construction projects, waste discharges and
dredging operations.
      Information on existing turbidity levels in the water
resources of the potential project area should be assembled.
Consideration needs to be given to the relationship between
turbidity levels and flow rates at the potential project site.

Prediction of Impacts: Prediction of impacts should include
consideration of anticipated changes in turbidity during both
the construction and operational phases of a project.   Mathematical approaches can be used to estimate increases in sediment
and turbidity from construction operations are found in many
reference sources, including Canter (1977).   Turbidity changes
can result from impoundment of water.   In summary, extensive
literature sources are available for identifying and quantifying
anticipated changes in turbidity levels resulting from construction and operation of water resources projects.

Functional Curve (Battelle Environmental Evaluation System, 1972):

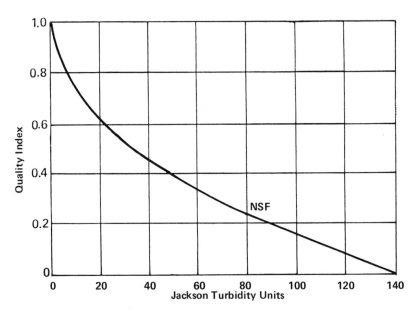

NSF = National Sanitation Foundation

Remarks: Consideration must be given to various measurement techniques for turbidity in assembling baseline information. Due to similarities in definitions and/or interpretation of information for turbidity, suspended solids, and suspended sediments, care must be exercised in assembling, predicting, and interpreting information on turbidity. Depending on data availability, the interdisciplinary team may want to use either turbidity or suspended solids as a variable in an assessment, but not both.

Data Sources:

    Battelle Environmental Evaluation System (1972).
    Canter (1977).

References:

    Battelle Dredging Impact Assessment Method (1974).
    Sawyer and McCarty (1967).

ACCOUNT: ENVIRONMENTAL QUALITY

CATEGORY: AQUATIC

SUBCATEGORY: WATER QUALITY

VARIABLE: SUSPENDED SOLIDS

Definition and Measurement of Baseline Conditions: Suspended
solids are solids contained in water which are not in solution;
they are distinguished from dissolved solids by laboratory filtration tests.   The unit of expression is mg/l.   Suspended
solids are comprised of settleable, floating, and nonsoluble
(colloidal suspension) components.   Suspended solids generally
contain both organic and inorganic (inert) substances.   One
property of suspended solids is that they impart to water the
characteristic of turbidity.   Suspended solids are of concern
due to their influence on esthetic quality, filtration, and
disinfection; and their potential impact on aquatic ecosystems.
In general, water containing greater concentrations of suspended solids is less desirable from an esthetic standpoint, is
more difficult and costly to filter, and requires higher chemical dosages for disinfection.   Excessive suspended solids can
be harmful to fish and other aquatic life by coating gills,
blanketing bottom organisms upon settling, and reducing solar
radiation intensity, thus effecting natural food chain relationships.
    Existing information on suspended solids concentrations
in surface watercourses in the potential project area should be
assembled.   Attention should be directed to seasonal variations
in suspended solids as related to flow variations.

Prediction of Impacts: Prediction of impacts should encompass
increases in suspended solids resulting from construction activities.   Consideration also needs to be given to anticipated
wastewater discharges resulting from usage of the created water
resources project, and from potential secondary impacts such
as population increases and industrial development.   Extensive
literature is available to enable quantification of anticipated
suspended solids concentrations and their resultant fate when
discharged into surface water bodies having different hydraulic
characteristics.   (Canter, 1977).   The influence of water
impoundment on suspended solids is also well documented in
available literature (U.S. Department of the Army, 1975).

106

Functional Curve: Use following concept from U.S. Department of the Army (1975):

Suspended Solids Concentration (mg/1)	Environmental Quality Category
4	Excellent
10	Good
15	Fair
20	Poor
35	Bad

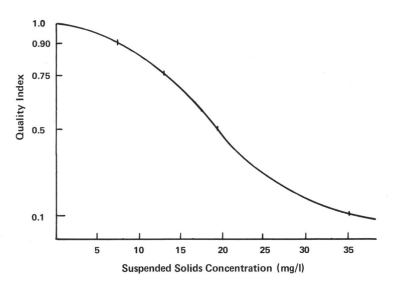

Remarks: Due to similarities in definitions and/or interpretation of information for turbidity, suspended solids, and suspended sediments, care must be exercised in assembling, predicting and interpreting information on suspended solids. Depending on data availability, the interdisciplinary team may want to use either turbidity or suspended solids as a variable in an assessment, but not both.

107

Data Sources:

Canter (1977).
U.S. Department of the Army (1975).

References:

Sawyer and McCarty (1967).

ACCOUNT: ENVIRONMENTAL QUALITY

CATEGORY: AQUATIC

SUBCATEGORY: WATER QUALITY

VARIABLE: WATER TEMPERATURE

Definition and Measurement of Baseline Conditions: Temperature
is the degree of hotness or coldness of water measured on a
definite scale such as degrees Centigrade ($^{\circ}$C) or degrees
Fahrenheit ($^{\circ}$F). Water temperature is a prime regulator of
natural processes within the aquatic environment. It governs
physiological functions in organisms and, acting directly or
indirectly in combination with other water quality constituents,
affects aquatic life with each change. Water temperature con-
trols spawning and hatching, regulates activity, and stimulates
or suppresses growth and development; it can cause death when
the water becomes heated or chilled too suddenly. Colder water
generally suppresses development; warmer water generally accel-
erates activity. Water temperature also influences numerous
physical and chemical reactions within the aquatic environment.
  Determination of baseline conditions for water temperature
includes assemblage of existing information on water temperature in the project area. Consideration should be given to
seasonal variations in water temperature as well as variations
of temperature with water depth.

Prediction of Impacts: Many activities associated with construction and operation of water resources projects can cause
changes in water temperature, and water impoundment can lead
to temperature changes at the water surface as well as at
various depths. Many excellent reference sources are available
for predicting water temperature changes resulting from construction and operation of water resources projects, including
Velz (1970), Markofsky and Harleman (1971), and Nemerow (1974).
All states have water quality standards for temperature, and
these standards can be used to assess the potential impact of
water resources projects. The functional curve shown below
indicates that the key concern is related to temperature variations from normal conditions. In accord with the observa-
tions for most fish, the functional curve implies less serious
effects for temperature changes that cool the natural environment than for those which warm the natural environment.

Functional Curve (Battelle Environmental Evaluation System, 1972):

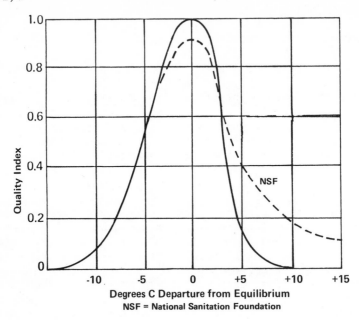

Degrees C Departure from Equilibrium

NSF = National Sanitation Foundation

Remarks: The interdisciplinary team must carefully consider the "natural" variations in water temperature within the project area.

Data Sources:

   Battelle Environmental Evaluation System (1972).
   Markofsky and Harleman (1971).
   Nemerow (1974).
   Velz (1970).

References:

   Battelle Dredging Impact Assessment Method (1974).
   Sawyer and McCarty (1967).
   U.S. Department of the Army (1975).

110

ACCOUNT: ENVIRONMENTAL QUALITY

CATEGORY: AQUATIC

SUBCATEGORY: WATER QUALITY

VARIABLE: DISSOLVED OXYGEN

Definition and Measurement of Baseline Conditions: Dissolved
oxygen is perhaps the most commonly employed parameter of
water quality. The solubility of atmospheric oxygen in fresh
water ranges from 14.6 mg/liter at 0°C to 7.1 mg/liter at
35°C under one atmosphere of pressure. Low levels of dissolved
oxygen adversely affect fish and other aquatic life, with the
total absence of dissolved oxygen leading to the development
of anaerobic conditions with attendant odor and esthetic problems. The oxygen requirements of fish vary with species and
age of fish. Cold water fish require higher dissolved oxygen
concentrations than do "coarse" fish (for example, carp and
pike), probably because the former are more active and predatory. The range of 3 to 6 mg/liter is the critical level of
dissolved oxygen for nearly all fish. Below 3 mg/liter,
further decreases in oxygen are important only insofar as the
development of local anaerobic conditions is concerned; the
major damage to fish and aquatic life will have already been
accomplished. Above 6 mg/liter, the major advantage of additional dissolved oxygen is as a reserve or buffer to handle
shock loads of high oxygen-demanding waste loads.
     Determination of baseline conditions for this variable
should include the assemblage of existing information on dissolved oxygen concentrations in surface water courses in the
project area. Consideration should be given to dissolved
oxygen variations as a function of season (water temperature)
and dissolved solids concentrations, if relevant, as in the
case of coastal waters.

Prediction of Impacts: Prediction of the impact of a potential project on dissolved oxygen should include consideration
of both the construction and operational phases. Numerous
mathematical models have been developed to enable prediction
of potential changes in dissolved oxygen as a result of water
impoundment, other hydraulic changes, and/or the introduction
of waste discharges. References for these models include
Velz (1970) and Nemerow (1974). Markofsky and Harlemen (1971)
provide predictive models for the influence of thermal stratification on dissolved oxygen concentrations in reservoirs.
All states have dissolved oxygen water quality standards, with
the numerical values varying depending on geographic location
and current/planned uses of the water body. The standards can
be used as one means of assessing the potential impact of a
project on dissolved oxygen.

<u>Functional Curve</u>:   (Battelle Environmental Evaluation System, 1972).

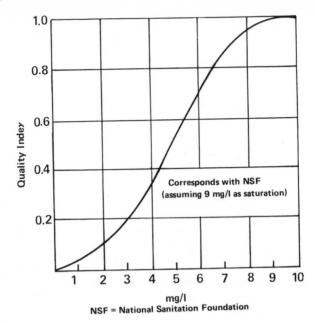

NSF = National Sanitation Foundation

<u>Remarks</u>:   Attention should be given to natural changes in dissolved oxygen within the project area.

<u>Data Sources</u>:

      Battelle Environmental Evaluation System (1972).
      Markofsky and Harleman (1971).
      Nemerow (1974).
      Velz (1970).

<u>References</u>:

      Battelle Dredging Impact Assessment Method (1974).
      Sawyer and McCarty (1967).

ACCOUNT: ENVIRONMENTAL QUALITY

CATEGORY: AQUATIC

SUBCATEGORY: WATER QUALITY

VARIABLE: BIOCHEMICAL OXYGEN DEMAND

Definition and Measurement of Baseline Conditions: Biochemical oxygen demand (BOD) is defined as the amount of oxygen (mg/1) required by bacteria while stabilizing decomposable organic matter under aerobic conditions. Typical test conditions include a five-day incubation period conducted at 20°C. Since BOD is an indirect measure of the amount of biologically degradable organic material, it is an indicator of the amount of dissolved oxygen that will be depleted from water during natural biological assimilation of organic pollutants. The BOD test is one of the most widely used tests in water quality evaluation.

Determination of baseline conditions for this variable would include aggregation of water quality information on BOD in the project area. Seasonal variations should be noted as well as historical trends in BOD concentrations. Consideration should be given to requirements of the Federal Water Pollution Control Act Amendments of 1972 (Public Law 92-500) relative to future reductions in organic waste loadings from point source discharges. In addition to considering the BOD concentrations in water, it may be necessary in describing the existing environment to aggregate total waste load inputs into the water resource, including those from point sources as well as non-point sources. Information useful for calculation of total BOD waste loads is contained in Canter (1977).

Prediction of Impacts: Prediction of the impacts of a potential project on the BOD should include consideration of the organic load from both the construction and operational phases, and encompass non-point sources as well as potential new point sources of waste discharge. Again, information is available in published literature, including Canter (1977), for calculating the total waste quantities to be introduced. Consideration should be given to the decomposition of organic materials in surface bodies of water resulting from the biological degradation processes. Mathematical models are available for predicting anticipated downstream concentrations of BOD. These models are described in Velz (1970) and Nemerow (1974). Consideration of the impact of water impoundment on BOD should also be included if the water resources project involves impoundment.

The rationale for the functional curve shown below is that BOD is important insofar as it promotes the depletion of

113

dissolved oxygen or the growth of undesirable benthic organisms.
In a slow sluggish stream or reservoir, a BOD of 5 mg/liter
might be sufficient to produce undesirable conditions, whereas
a swift mountain stream might easily handle 30 mg/liter of BOD
or more without significant deleterious effects. This is
because swift-moving streams have a greater capacity for reaeration and for preventing the accumulation of high BOD materials
in bottom sediments. The National Sanitation Foundation functional curve falls between the functional curves provided for
the two extreme conditions described above (Battelle Environmental Evaluation System, 1972).

Functional Curve: (Battelle Environmental Evaluation System,
1972)

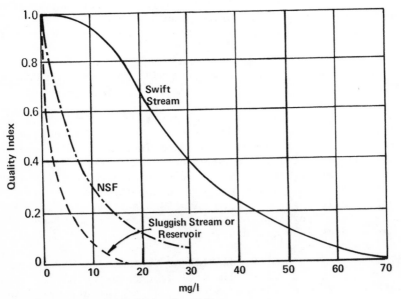

NSF = National Sanitation Foundation

Remarks: It is becoming increasingly important to give consideration to non-point sources of pollution in accounting for
the BOD in watercourses.

Data Sources:

> Battelle Environmental Evaluation System (1972).
> Canter (1977).
> Nemerow (1974).
> Velz (1970).

114

References:

Sawyer and McCarty (1967).
U.S. Department of the Army (1975).

ACCOUNT: ENVIRONMENTAL QUALITY

CATEGORY: AQUATIC

SUBCATEGORY: WATER QUALITY

VARIABLE: DISSOLVED SOLIDS

Definition and Measurement of Baseline Conditions: Total dissolved solids (TDS) are the aggregate of carbonates, bicarbonates, chlorides, sulfates, phosphates, nitrates, and other
salts of calcium, magnesium, sodium, potassium, and other substances. Total dissolved solids are separated from suspended
solids through laboratory filtration techniques. The unit of
measurement is mg/l. Total dissolved solids are of concern
due to their effect on palatability and their potential for
causing unfavorable physiological reactions. Highly mineral-
ized waters are also unsuitable for many industrial applications, and they may be limited in their potential use for
irrigation.

Determination of the baseline conditions for this variable
would involve the assemblage of existing information on TDS in
the waters of interest at the potential project site. Consideration should be given to variations in TDS concentrations as
a function of variations in streamflows.

Prediction of Impacts: Prediction of impacts should include
consideration of both construction and operational phase
impacts, although the primary focus for this variable should
probably be related to operational phase concerns. Quantification of anticipated TDS to be introduced as a result of a potential project can be made through the application of various
unit waste generation factors as described by Canter (1977).
Prediction of the fate of dissolved solids once they reach
surface water courses can be accomplished through the application of mathematical models based on the principles of dilution.
Consideration may be appropriate relative to the chemical form
of the dissolved solids and potential chemical precipitation
which could occur as a function of changes in pH and temperature.
Particular consideration should be given to the potential
build-up of TDS as a result of evaporation losses from water
impoundment projects.

All states have water quality standards for dissolved
solids which are a function of geographical location, natural
sources of TDS, and current/potential use of the water resource.
Standards can be used to assess the potential impacts of water
resources projects. The functional curve shown below indicates
that environmental quality relative to TDS exhibits a decreasing relationship, that is, with increasing TDS concentrations,
the environmental quality decreases. The functional curve as

116

developed recognizes that some finite concentration of TDS is
essential at the lower extreme in order to achieve chemical
equilibrium within water.

Functional Curve (Battelle Environmental Evaluation System, 1972):

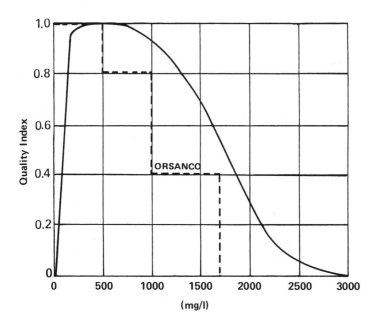

Remarks: Attention should be given to natural variations in
TDS within the project area.

Data Sources:

    Battelle Environmental Evaluation System (1972).
    Canter (1977).

References:

    Battelle Dredging Impact Assessment Method (1974).
    Nemerow (1970).
    Sawyer and McCarty (1967).
    U.S. Department of the Army (1975).
    Velz (1970).

ACCOUNT: ENVIRONMENTAL QUALITY

CATEGORY: AQUATIC

SUBCATEGORY: WATER QUALITY

VARIABLE: INORGANIC NITROGEN

Definition and Measurement of Baseline Conditions: Nitrogen,
along with carbon and phosphorus is one of the three major
elemental nutrients needed to sustain aquatic life. It is
normally measured in mg/l. Specifically, inorganic nitrogen
primarily in the form of nitrates and ammonia is available for
incorporation into the aquatic food cycle. Organic nitrogen
becomes available usually only after conversion to inorganic
forms by bacterial action. Industrial and municipal wastes
and fertilizer residues in agricultural runoff are the major
sources of inorganic nitrogen in surface waters.

    Determination of baseline conditions for this variable
would include aggregation of water quality information on inorganic nitrogen in the project area. Seasonal variations
should be noted as well as historical trends in inorganic nitrogen concentrations. Consideration should be given to requirements of the Federal Water Pollution Control Act Amendments of
1972 (P.L. 92-500) relative to future reductions in nitrogen
loadings from point source discharges. In addition to considering inorganic nitrogen concentrations in water, it may be
necessary in describing the existing environment to aggregate
total nitrogen inputs into the water resource, including those
from point sources as well as non-point sources. Information
useful for calculation of total inorganic nitrogen loads is
contained in Canter (1977).

Prediction of Impacts: Prediction of the impacts of a potential project on inorganic nitrogen concentrations should
include consideration of the inorganic nitrogen loads from
both the construction and operational phases, and encompass
non-point sources as well as potential new point sources of
waste discharge. Again, information is available from published
literature, including Canter (1977), for calculating the total
waste quantities to be introduced. Consideration should be
given to possible chemical changes and biological conversion
of inorganic nitrogen forms in surface bodies of water. Mathematical models are available for predicting anticipated downstream concentrations of inorganic nitrogen. (Battelle Dredging
Impact Assessment Method, 1974). Consideration of the impact
of water impoundment on inorganic nitrogen concentrations
should also be included if the water resources project involves
impoundment.

118

The functional curve shown below is based on the premise that there is an optimum range of inorganic nitrogen concentrations, with environmental quality decreasing for actual concentrations above or below the optimum range. As in the case of phosphorus, small quantities of nitrogen are essential to support aquatic ecosystems; below approximately 0.30 mg/l inorganic nitrogen (expressed as N) is usually a nitrogen-deficient range. Concentrations above 1.0 mg/l of inorganic nitrogen as N may be less than optimum. Inorganic nitrogen concentrations of 10 mg/l or more as N may become inhibiting to biological processes (Battelle Environmental Evaluation System, 1972).

Functional Curve: (Battelle Environmental Evaluation System, 1972)

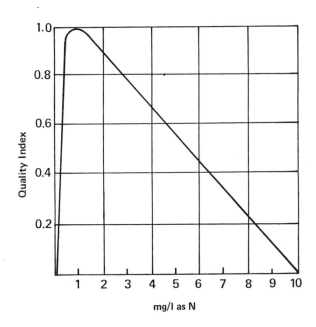

mg/l as N

Remarks: The shape of the above functional curve is considered to be generally applicable, although the N concentration for maximum EQ may vary from region to region.

Data Sources:

Battelle Dredging Impact Assessment Method (1974).
Battelle Environmental Evaluation System (1972).
Canter (1977).

119

References:

Sawyer and McCarty (1967).
U.S. Department of the Army (1975).

ACCOUNT: ENVIRONMENTAL QUALITY

CATEGORY: AQUATIC

SUBCATEGORY: WATER QUALITY

VARIABLE: INORGANIC PHOSPHATE

Definition and Measurement of Baseline Conditions: Phosphorus,
along with nitrogen and carbon, is one of the three major elemental nutrients needed to sustain aquatic life. It is normally measured in mg/l. Various forms of inorganic phosphorus
have been the most commonly discussed contributors to the
general problem of eutrophication. Sources of phosphorus in
surface waters include domestic and industrial wastes and agricultural runoff containing commercial fertilizer components.
     Determination of baseline conditions for this variable
would include aggregation of water quality information on
inorganic phosphates in the project area. Seasonal variations
should be noted as well as historical trends in inorganic
phosphate concentrations. Consideration should be given to
requirements of the Federal Water Pollution Control Act Amendments of 1972 (PL 92-500) relative to future reductions in
organic phosphate loadings from point source discharges. In
addition to considering the inorganic phosphate concentrations
in water, it may be necessary in describing the existing environment to aggregate total phosphate inputs into the water
resource, including those from point sources as well as non-
point sources. Information useful for calculation of total
inorganic phosphate loads is contained in Canter (1977).

Prediction of Impacts: Predicition of the impacts of a potential project on inorganic phosphates should include consideration of the waste load from both the construction and operational phases, and encompass non-point sources as well as
potential new point sources of inorganic phosphate discharge.
Again, information is available in published literature,
including Canter (1977), for calculating the total inorganic
phosphate quantity to be introduced. The fate of inorganic
phosphate in water is dependent upon biological processes as
well as chemical reactions. Mathematical models are available
for predicting anticipated downstream concentrations of inorganic phosphate (Battelle Dredging Impact Assessment Method,
1974). Consideration of the impact of water impoundment on
inorganic phosphate concentrations should also be included if
the water resources project involves impoundment.

     The rationale for the functional curve shown below is
that although the concentration of inorganic phosphate that will
produce problems varies with the nature of the aquatic environment and the levels of other nutrients, most relatively

uncontaminated lake areas are known to have surface waters that contain 0.001 to 0.003 mg/1 total phosphorus expressed as P. These areas are considered to be nutrient deficient. Above 0.02 mg/1 P is the region of potential algal bloom. Above 0.10 mg/1 P, water is excessively enriched (Battelle Environmental Evaluation System, 1972).

Functional Curve (Battelle Environmental Evaluation System, 1972):

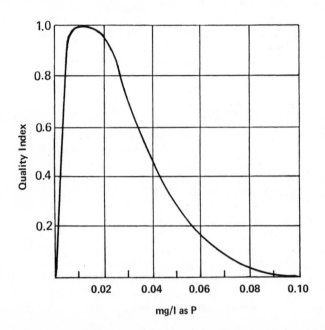

Remarks: The shape of the above functional curve is considered to be generally applicable, although the P concentration for maximum EQ may vary from region to region.

Data Sources:

    Battelle Dredging Impact Assessment Method (1974).
    Battelle Environmental Evaluation System (1972).
    Canter (1977).

References:

    Sawyer and McCarty (1967).
    U.S. Department of the Army (1975).

ACCOUNT: ENVIRONMENTAL QUALITY

CATEGORY: AQUATIC

SUBCATEGORY: WATER QUALITY

VARIABLE: SALINITY

Definition and Measurement of Baseline Conditions: Salinity
is defined as the total solids in water after all carbonates
have been converted to oxides, all bromides and iodides have
been replaced by chlorides, and all organic matter has been
oxidized. The unit of expression of salinity is generally
grams per kilogram or parts per thousand. Salinity is an important variable in coastal and estuarine waters, and is of particular concern in that changes in salinity can cause changes
in the aquatic ecosystem relative to the types and relative
abundance of organisms. Salinity should be utilized as an
impact assessment variable for all water resources projects
associated with coastal waters and estuaries.
    Determination of baseline conditions for this variable
would include assemblage of existing information on salinity
values in the vicinity of the project area. Consideration
needs to be given to diurnal and seasonal variations of salinity, as well as to variations relative to water depth at a
given location.

Prediction of Impacts: Prediction of impacts should primarily
be focused on possible changes in salinity concentrations
resulting from construction and operation of the project. Predictive techniques are available, with the approach related to
the hydraulic characteristics of the coastal zone and/or
estuary. Reference sources include Velz (1970) and Nemerow
(1974).
    The functional curve shown below is based on the premise
that changes from normally occurring levels of salinity represent a decrease in environmental equality. Changes can cause
increases or decreases in salinity, depending upon the particular water resources project.

Functional Curve:

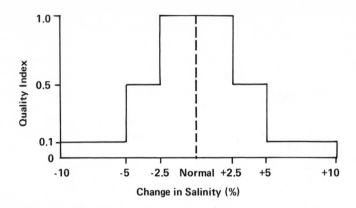

Change in Salinity (%)

Remarks: Particular attention needs to be addressed to determining "normal" salinity ranges for the project area. Unique hydraulic modelling may be required for impact prediction.

Data Sources:

    Nemerow (1974).
    Velz (1970).

References:

    Battelle Dredging Impact Assessment Method (1974).

ACCOUNT: ENVIRONMENTAL QUALITY

CATEGORY: AQUATIC

SUBCATEGORY: WATER QUALITY

VARIABLE: IRON AND MANGANESE

Definition and Measurement of Baseline Conditions: Iron and
manganese are transition metals which can create difficulties
in water supplies due to certain undesirable consequences.
Both iron and manganese interfere with laundering operations,
impart objectionable stains to plumbing fixtures, and cause
difficulties in distribution systems by supporting growth of
iron bacteria.   Iron also imparts a taste to water which is
detectable at low concentrations.   For these reasons the U.S.
Public Health Service Drinking Water Standards recommend that
public water supplies should not contain more than 0.3 mg/l
of iron or 0.05 mg/l of manganese.
     The primary source of iron and manganese in surface waters
as well as groundwaters is from the dissolution of these metals
from various soils (Sawyer and McCarty, 1967).   Under aerobic
conditions in water, dissolved iron and manganese, may be precipitated through the formation of ferric oxide, ferric hydrox-
ide and manganese dioxide.   Of major concern in surface water
supplies is the fact that previously precipitated iron and
manganese can be resolubilized under anaerobic conditions.
The iron and manganese problem in impounded surface supplies
has been correlated with reservoirs that stratify, occurring
when anaerobic conditions develop in the hypolimnion.   Soluble
iron and manganese released from bottom muds is contained in
the waters of the hypolimnion until the impoundment overturns;
and at that time they will be distributed throughout the reservoir.   If the intake for the reservoir is in the hypolimnion,
then waters can be released downstream containing excessive
concentrations of ferrous iron and manganese in the +2 oxida-
tion state.
     Measurement of this variable for the existing environment
would include aggregation of water quality information on iron
and manganese in the project area.   Seasonal variations should
be noted as well as historical trends in iron and manganese
concentrations.   If unique sources of iron and manganese exist
within the watershed, for example, from industrial point source
discharges, then these sources should also be documented as a
part of describing the existing environment.   If the major
sources of iron and manganese are from natural soil runoff,
then this should also be established.

Prediction of Impacts: Prediction of the impacts of a potential project on iron and manganese concentrations should

include primary focus of attention on the operational phases of the project, particularly if water is being impounded and the possibility for thermal stratification exist. Extensive information has been published regarding the effects of impoundment on iron and manganese cycling (Ortolano, 1973). Mathematical models for predicting anticipated iron and manganese concentrations in reservoirs as well as at downstream locations are under development at the current time.

The functional curve shown below is based upon the premise that environmental quality decreases as iron and manganese concentrations increase above the Public Health Service Drinking Water Standards. Qualitative judgment would have to be exercised regarding the assessment of periodic fluctuations in iron and manganese as well as long-term changes in these transition metals in the water environment.

Functional Curve

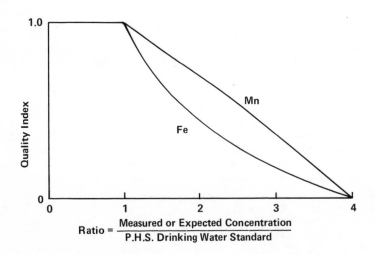

Remarks: The chemical species can become very complex and difficult to understand without the aid of a chemist.

Data Sources:

    Ortolano (1973).
    Sawyer and McCarty (1967).

Reference:

    Standard Methods (1976).

ACCOUNT: ENVIRONMENTAL QUALITY

CATEGORY: AQUATIC

SUBCATEGORY: WATER QUALITY

VARIABLE: TOXIC SUBSTANCES

Definition and Measurement of Baseline Conditions: Many potential toxic substances can exist within the aquatic environment.
Wastes containing concentrations of heavy metals (mercury,
copper, silver, lead, nickel, cobalt, arsenic, cadmium,
chromium, and others), either individually or in combination
may be toxic to aquatic organisms and, thus, have a severe
impact on aquatic ecosystems. Other toxic substances include
pesticides, ammonia-ammonium compounds, cyanides, sulfides,
flourides, and chlorinated organic compounds. Pesticides are
treated as a separate variable.

The bioassay test can be used to indicate the concentration in mg/l at which toxic compounds will not cause an appar-
ent effect upon test organisms. However, long-term effects
of toxic substances may have more subtle changes such as
reduced growth, lowered fertility, altered physiology, and
induced abnormal behavior patterns; and these may cause more
disastrous effects than the existence of a species. Also,
biological magnification and storage of toxic residues of
polluting substances in aquatic organisms may cause serious
after-effects. For all these reasons, and as a practical
matter, toxic compounds, if they could be detected in natural
waters by modern water quality analysis methods, may render
water undesirable for propagation of healthy aquatic life.

Determination of baseline conditions for this variable
would include aggregation of water quality information on any
of the toxic substances delineated above that might be occurring in the project area. If the data is available historical
trends in the concentrations of potentially toxic substances
should be noted. In addition to considering existing concentrations in water, with the probability being that there will
be little existing information on the above-listed substances,
the interdisciplinary team should consider if there are any
existing point sources of toxic substances within the watershed. This information could be procured from the state water
quality agency.

Prediction of Impacts: Prediction of the impacts of a potential project on toxic substances should include consideration
of the possible introduction of toxic materials from both the
construction and operational phases. Consideration should be
given to the environmental cycles of various toxic materials;
that is, do they tend to precipitate from solution, be lost to

the atmosphere through volatilization, or be taken up in various aquatic forms. Extensive information on the environmental fate of various toxic substances can be procured through literature sources associated with radioactive wastes, since many radionuclides of concern are isotopes of the above toxic metals. Mathematical models are not generally available for predicting anticipated downstream concentrations of numerous toxic substances. One particular point to be noted is the possible synergistic or antagonistic interactions between mixed substances which may cause different effects than those associated with respective toxic substances considered separately.

Functional Curve: None is available. A functional curve concept similar to that for the pesticides environmental variable could be used (Battelle Environmental Evaluation System, 1972).

Remarks: This environmental variable groups together all potentially toxic substances with the exception of pesticides. If several toxic or potentially toxic substances exist in the project area, consideration should be given to their separate inclusion in the assessment.

Data Sources:

Battelle Environmental Evaluation System (1972).

References:

U.S. Department of the Army (1975).

CATEGORY: AQUATIC

SUBCATEGORY: WATER QUALITY

VARIABLE: PESTICIDES

Definition and Measurement of Baseline Conditions: Pesticides is a collective term which includes insecticides, herbicides, and algaecides which may be applied to land or water in order to control undesirable flora and fauna. The effects of pesticides vary widely from one pesticide to another, as well as from species to species of aquatic plant or animal.

Determination of baseline conditions for this variable would include aggregation of water quality information in mg/1 on various pesticides in the project area. Seasonal variations should be noted as well as historical trends in pesticide concentrations. Since pesticides primarily originate from land application, it may be necessary to assemble information on the previous history of pesticide usage in the watershed.

Prediction of Impacts: Prediction of the impacts of a potential project on pesticide concentrations should include consideration of the potential introduction of pesticides during the construction phase as well as the operational phase. The fate of pesticide materials in surface water-courses can be estimated through consideration of published information regarding transport. Mathematical models are generally not available for predicting anticipated downstream concentrations of pesticides, nor for predicting the potential impacts of water impoundment on pesticides.

Because maximum permissible concentrations vary so widely for pesticides, and because it would be too unwieldy to have a separate functional curve for each pesticide, the functional curve shown below is based on the ratio of the existing (or predicted) concentration of a given pesticide to its respective maximum permissible concentration (Battelle Environmental Evaluation System, 1972). If only one pesticide is present the functional curve is used directly. In this case, the **quality index varies linearly from 1.0 (zero pesticide) to 0** when the existing or predicted concentration reaches the maximum permissible concentration ratio is not a satisfactory surrogate, nor can concentration ratios be meaningfully added. To account for multiple pesticides, the following can be utilized:

$$QI = \left(\frac{\sum\limits_{i=1}^{N} QI_i}{N} \right) (0.9)^N$$

where
    QI = Overall quality index for pesticides
    QI_i = Quality index for pesticide i obtained from functional curve
    N = Number of pesticides.

Functional Curve (Battelle Environmental Evaluation System, 1972):

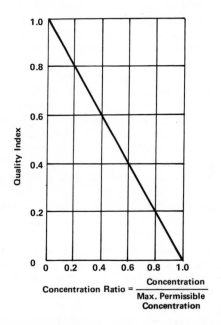

Remarks: If it is determined that usage of two or three pesticides are dominant in the project area, the interdisciplinary team may want to consider their separate inclusion in the assessment.

Data Sources:

Battelle Environmental Evaluation System (1972).

References:

Battelle Dredging Impact Assessment Method (1974).

130

ACCOUNT: ENVIRONMENTAL QUALITY

CATEGORY: AQUATIC

SUBCATEGORY: WATER QUALITY

VARIABLE: FECAL COLIFORMS

Definition and Measurement of Baseline Conditions: Water can
act as a vehicle for the spread of disease. The presence of
coliform organisms in water is regarded as evidence of fecal
contamination since these organisms have their origin in the
intestinal tract of humans and other warm-blooded animals.
The necessity of coliform tests for water supplies has declined
somewhat since water treatment plants effectively remove most
of the disease-causing bacteria by treatment and disinfection.
However, fecal coliform tests continue to be important because
of recreational usage of water involving body-contact, and
because of implications that viral diseases can be transmitted
through the fecal contamination of water supplies. Indirect
routes such as the contamination of food with fecally-
contaminated irrigation water, and accumulation of contaminants
by oysters, clams, and mussels from fecally-contaminated
marine waters, continue to be areas of concern.
    Determination of baseline conditions for this variable
would include aggregation of water quality information on
fecal coliform concentrations in the project area. Concentrations are expressed in most probable number (MPN) per 100 ml.
Seasonal variations should be noted as well as historical
trends in fecal coliform levels. Consideration should be
given to the requirements of the Federal Water Pollution Control Act Amendments of 1972 (PL 92-500) relative to future
reductions in bacterial loadings from point source discharges.
In addition to considering fecal coliform concentrations in
water, it may be necessary in describing the existing environment to aggregate the total waste load input into the water
resource, including wastes from point sources as well as non-
point sources. Information useful for calculating total fecal
coliform loadings is contained in Canter (1977).

Prediction of Impacts: Prediction of the impacts of a potential project on fecal coliform concentrations should include
consideration of the loadings from both the construction and
operational phases, and encompass non-point sources as well as
potential new point sources of waste discharge. Again, information is available in published literature, including Canter
(1977), for calculating the fecal coliform quantities to be
introduced. Consideration should be given to the natural die-
away of these organisms in surface bodies of water, and it may
be necessary to consider the possibility of after-growth

following discharge into certain aquatic conditions. Mathematical models are available for predicting anticipated downstream fecal coliform concentrations, with these models described in Velz (1970) and Nemerow (1974). Consideration of the impact of water impoundment on fecal coliform concentrations should also be included if the potential project involves impoundment.

The coliform scale on the functional curve shown below is logarithmic and measured in the conventional units of most probable number per 100 ml (MPN/100 ml). The rationale for the functional curve is that the U.S. Public Health Service Drinking Water Standard is one organism per 100 ml (10^0) while the fecal coliform concentration in a raw sewage may be 10^6 organisms or more per 100 ml (Battelle Environmental Evaluation System, 1972). Value functions developed by the National Sanitation Foundation (NSF) and the Ohio River Sanitation Commission (ORSANCO) are also shown. The function developed in the Battelle Environmental Evaluation System is midway between the extremes suggested by the NSF and ORSANCO. The functional curve is S-shaped to reflect the relative inconsequential nature of unit changes at the lower and upper ends of the scale, and the critical nature of the range from 10^2 to 10^4 MPN/100 ml.

Functional Curve (Battelle Environmental Evaluation System, 1972):

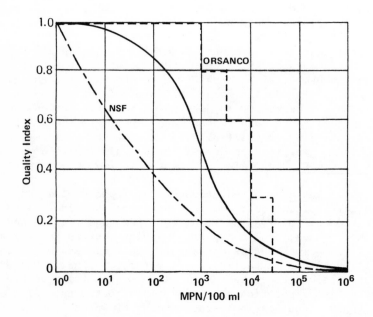

Remarks: If water quality data are available on specific disease-causing organisms, the interdisciplinary team may want to consider using it in lieu of data on fecal coliforms.

Data Sources:

Battelle Environmental Evaluation System (1972).
Canter (1977).
Nemerow (1974).
Velz (1970).

References:

U.S. Department of the Army (1975).

ACCOUNT: ENVIRONMENTAL QUALITY

CATEGORY: AQUATIC

SUBCATEGORY: WATER QUALITY

VARIABLE: STREAM ASSIMILATIVE CAPACITY

Definition and Measurement of Baseline Conditions: Stream assimilative capacity (allowable waste loading) represents the natural self-purification capacity of a stream subjected to organic waste loadings. Due to natural reaeration and other related hydraulic and environmental characteristics, streams can receive organic waste and biologically decompose it without the creation of undesirable conditions relative to dissolved oxygen concentrations. The unit of measurement for stream assimilative capacity is pounds BOD per day.

Determination of baseline conditions for this variable includes an estimation of the allowable waste loading, in the vicinity of the project area, which could be received by the stream and yet not create undesirable consequences. Several references provide calculation procedures for determining allowable waste loading (stream assimilative capacity), including Canter (1977), Velz (1970), and Nemerow (1974). Consideration should be given to changes in the stream assimilative capacity with season and flow conditions in the potential project area.

Prediction of Impacts: Prediction of the impacts of a water resources project should include consideration of any changes in the hydraulics of the stream and the exposed area of water which would result from project construction and implementation. It is possible for water resources projects to either increase or decrease stream assimilative capacity. Again, the basic mathematical relationships utilized to determine allowable waste loading for the existing environment could be utilized for projecting the anticipated future stream assimilative capacity with changed hydraulic characteristics. Particular consideration needs to be given to this variable when water is to be impounded, since water impoundment causes fairly significant decreases in allowable waste loadings. The functional curve shown below is based on the premise that decreases in stream assimilative capacity lead to decreases in environmental quality.

Functional Curve

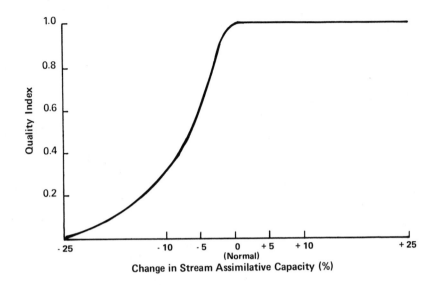

Change in Stream Assimilative Capacity (%)

Remarks: Information from state-developed waste load alloca-
tion studies will be useful in establishing the normal stream
assimilative capacity for the project area.

Data Sources:

  Canter (1977).
  Nemerow (1974).
  Velz (1970).

References:

  Battelle Dredging Impact Assessment Method (1974).

135

ACCOUNT: ENVIRONMENTAL QUALITY

CATEGORY: AQUATIC

SUBCATEGORY: WATER QUANTITY

VARIABLE: STREAM FLOW VARIATION

Definition and Measurement of Baseline Conditions: The veloc-
ity of flow and total discharge are extremely important to
aquatic organisms in a number of ways, including the transport
of nutrients and organic food past those organisms attached
to stationary surfaces; the transport of plankton and benthos
as drift, which in turn serves as food for higher organisms;
and the addition of oxygen to water through surface aeration.
Sediments are moved downstream and may be transported as bed
load.   Sediments are often associated with major nutrients,
such as nitrogen and phosphorus, and these nutrients may be
released downstream.   Natural flow variations, as well as
flow variations caused by man, are critical factors governing
stream development.   If the pattern of stream flow variation
is changed markedly from that which is natural, subsequent
destruction of the stream may result.
    Determination of baseline conditions for this variable
will involve analysis of existing flow information from the
potential project area with regard to daily maximum and minimum flows, as well as the rate of change of flow from maximum
to minimum.   In the functional curves utilized below, the
time periods of flow change are expressed as 2 hours, 12 hours,
and 24 hours (Battelle Environmental Evaluation System, 1972).

Prediction of Impacts: Prediction of the impact of a potential water resources project on this variable would involve
hydraulics-related calculations to estimate changes in daily
maximum to minimum flows, as well as the time period over
which these flow changes are anticipated to occur.   Numerous
mathematical models are available for accomplishing these
predictions.   The attached table from the Urban Institute
(1976) provides a comparison of techniques used to estimate
changes in stream flow.
    In order to assess the impact of stream flow variations,
four functional curves are presented (Battelle Environmental
Evaluation System, 1972).   The basic principle employed in the
functional curves was that the more rapid and extensive the
stream flow variation, the worse the condition from an environmental quality viewpoint.   The overall functional curve is
structured around three essential factors and requires four
separate functional curves to present.   The three factors are:

136

	Types of Water Bodies	Watershed	Computing Requirements
Rational Method	Streams	Less than $\sim$5 mi^2	Compilation of precipitation tables, manual computation
Flood Frequency Analysis	Streams, lakes estuaries	No limit	Access to a digital computer desirable to perform regression analyses and to fit flood data into the accepted distributional form
Hydrocomp Simulation Program (HSP)	Streams, lakes reservoirs	No limit	Designed for use on the IBM 360 or 370 computer

	Input	Cost	Output
Rational Method	Precipitation depth-frequency-duration tables, percent impervious grond cover in the watershed	Relatively low	Peak stream flow for storms of various degrees of severity
Flood Frequency Analysis	Stream flow records for gauged streams, watershed size and slope, average annual precipitation, and land use for numerous watersheds for several years	Low-medium (since additional time-consuming lculations are necessary)	Peak stream flow for storms of various degrees of severity
Hydrocomp Simulation Program (HSP)	Hourly precipitation and evaporation; extent, location and type type of sewerage and ground cover	Approximately $10/ac for small watersheds, considerably less for	Continuous stream flow hydrographs for as many points in the watershed and for as

Input	Cost	Output
in watershed; channel configuration (for snowfall--daily and maximum and minimum temperatures, point, wind velocity, radiation and cloud cover desirable)	large ones	many years as desired

	Accuracy
Rational Method	Some reports of errors as great as 50% in reproducing past events
Flood Frequency Analysis	High for reproducing past events once it has been calibrated; unknown for future events
Hydrocomp Simulation Program (HSP)	High for reproducing past events and "good" for future events as rated by the developers, although no documentation is available

(a) The magnitude of the stream flow variation over a year expressed as the ratio, Daily Max/Daily Min; Four discrete values for the flow ratio are employed

	Daily Max/Daily Min
1	2:1
2	2:1 - 10:1
3	10:1 - 50:1
4	50:1

(b) The number of days per year (expressed as a percentage of 365 on which the above flow ratios occur)

(c) The predominant period of time over which the flow changes from a maximum to a minimum value or vice versa; three discrete time periods are employed

Period	t, hours
1	2
2	12
3	24

With data on the above three factors, the four functional curves are used to generate an overall QI score:

$$QI = \sum_{i=1}^{n} f_i$$

where n = the number of curves needed to account for the total range of flow variation, and

f_i = QI value for ith. range of flow variation.

Functional Curves (Battelle Environmental Evaluation System, 1972):

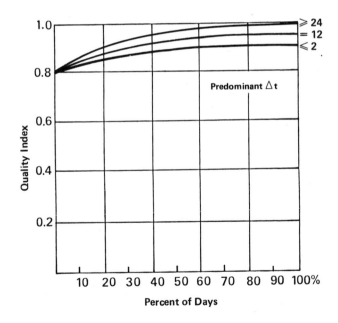

STREAM FLOW VARIATIONS, DAILY MAX/MIN ≤ 2:1

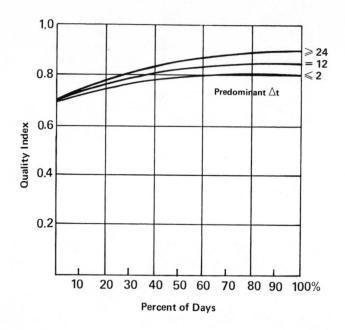

STREAM FLOW VARIATIONS, DAILY MAX/MIN ≤ 10:1

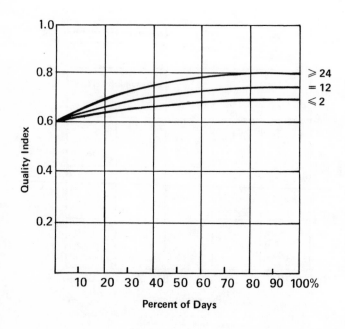

STREAM FLOW VARIATIONS, MAX/MIN ≤ 50:1

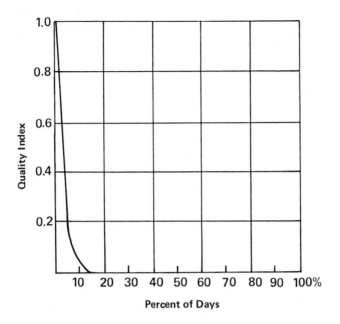

STREAM FLOW VARIATIONS, MAX/MIN > 50:1

Remarks: Extensive data analyses and predictions will be required in order to incorporate this variable in the assessment.

Data Sources:

Battelle Environmental Evaluation System (1972).
Urban Institute (1976).

References:

U.S. Department of the Army (1975).

ACCOUNT: ENVIRONMENTAL QUALITY

CATEGORY: AQUATIC

SUBCATEGORY: WATER QUANTITY

VARIABLE: BASIN HYDROLOGIC LOSS

Definition and Measurement of Baseline Conditions: Basin hydrologic loss is the ratio of man-made losses of water to the annual natural discharge from a watershed. Man-made losses occur from evaporative losses from artificial water surfaces, and from consumptive losses of water via use for municipal, industrial, or agricultural purposes. The annual natural discharge is determined by adding to the average annual discharge the existing evaporative and other net water losses due to previous developments in the basin. The key concern is the possible impacts on aquatic ecosystems in the project area.

Determination of baseline conditions for this variable would involve the assemblage of existing information on annual discharges at the mouth of the river in the project area, or discharges flowing past the project area, depending upon the spatial boundaries of the project. Consumptive losses of water in the basin would have to be estimated as well as existing water losses from evaporation and evapotranspiration.

Prediction of Impacts: Prediction of the impact of a potential water resources project should be primarily focused on the operational phase of the project and possible increases in evaporation and transpiration resulting therefrom. Evaporation could be decreased where slow-moving streams are changing to more rapid-flowing systems as a result of clearing and snagging or channelization projects. Future increases in water usage as a result of the project should be estimated, and consumptive losses anticipated to occur should be projected.

The functional curve shown below is based on a decreasing environmental quality as basin hydrologic loss increases. The basin hydrologic loss, as defined by the ratio described above, will range from 0 to 2.0. The following criteria are used (Battelle Environmental Evaluation System, 1972):

As the basin hydrologic loss rate increases from 0, the environmental impact of the first units of water lost are less adverse than losses of each subsequent unit; hence, the value function should have a gradual slope in the region of zero loss.

Once a major fraction, say 90 percent, of the available natural discharge is lost through "basin

development," the remaining water is extremely cru-
cial and the marginal impact of the loss of each
additional unit of water is more serious than the
last. This suggests a value function having a steep
slope where the ratio approaches 1.0.

Functional Curve (Battelle Environmental Evaluation System,
1972):

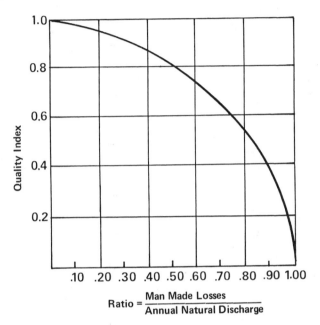

Remarks: Consideration needs to be given to normal variations
in the discharge under baseline conditions.

Data Sources:

    Battelle Environmental Evaluation System (1972).

Reference:

    Battelle Dredging Impact Assessment Method (1974).

ACCOUNT: ENVIRONMENTAL QUALITY

CATEGORY: AQUATIC

SUBCATEGORY: CRITICAL COMMUNITY RELATIONSHIPS

VARIABLE: SPECIES DIVERSITY

Definition and Measurement of Baseline Conditions: Ratios
between the number of species and abundant species are defined
as species diversity indices. Aquatic species diversity is
used as a correlation to community stability. A low species
diversity is considered characteristic of a successional stage
or an extreme environmental condition.
    The value function and the techniques for evaluating
aquatic species diversity are the same as those used for terrestrial species diversity (in Terrestrial/Critical Community
Relationships). However, in this case the benthic invertebrates are used as the indicator group. Again, a variety of
aquatic habitats are sampled and the mean number of species
per 1000 individuals is used as the parameter value.

Prediction of Impacts: Changes resulting from the proposed
project may be predicted by measuring this parameter in similar
habitats where projects are completed and operating.

Functional Curve (Battelle Environmental Evaluation System,
1972):

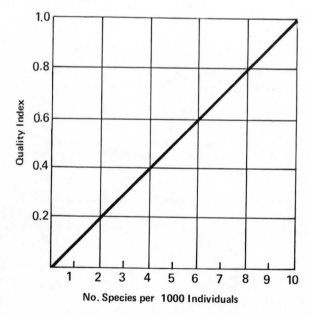

Remarks: Species diversity tends to be low in physically controlled systems and high in biologically controlled systems.

Data Sources:

Battelle Environmental Evaluation System (1972).

References:

Bechtel and Copeland (1970).
Patten (1962).
Ransom and Dorris (1972).
Wilhm (1970).

AIR VARIABLES

ACCOUNT: ENVIRONMENTAL QUALITY

CATEGORY: AIR

SUBCATEGORY: QUALITY

VARIABLE: CARBON MONOXIDE

Definition and Measurement of Baseline Conditions: Carbon monoxide is a colorless, odorless, tasteless gas formed by the combustion of carbonaceous fuels. It is the most widely distributed and commonly occurring air pollutant. On a tonnage basis, the total emissions of carbon monoxide into the atmosphere exceed those of all other air pollutants combined. The majority of atmospheric carbon monoxide is produced by the incomplete combustion of carbonaceous materials used as fuels for vehicles, space heating and industrial processing. Ambient air quality standards exist for carbon monoxide. Adverse health effects have been observed with carbon monoxide concentrations of 12-17 milligrams per cubic meter (mg/M^3) for 8 hours. The Federal ambient air quality standards for carbon monoxide are as follows:

> Maximum 8-hr concentration not to be exceeded more than once a year = 10 mg/M^3 or 9 ppm.
> Maximum 1-hr concentration not to be exceeded more than once a year = 40 mg/M^3 or 35 ppm.
> Carbon monoxide can be measured continuously through the use of non-dispersive infrared spectroscopy.

Prediction of Impacts: The primary sources of carbon monoxide in relation to water resources projects are emissions from vehicular traffic, including automobiles and construction equipment. To measure this variable in the existing environment the interdisciplinary team should assemble known information on carbon monoxide concentrations in the project area, as well as summarize emission inventory data for this pollutant in the vicinity. Existing carbon monoxide concentrations can be compared with Federal and state ambient air quality standards. Prediction of impacts will involve consideration of the potential contribution of the project to the regional emission inventory for carbon monoxide. This can be called mesoscale impact assessment. Carbon monoxide emission factors for vehicles and land clearing activities can be utilized, with these being found in "Air Pollution Emission Factors" (1973). Contributions of the potential project to the emission inventory can be expressed on a percentage basis, and the functional curve shown below can be utilized. Consideration would also need to be given to carbon monoxide which might arise from secondary growth in the project area, including population increases as well as industrial development.

If the percentage increase in the carbon monoxide emission inventory is greater than 5%, or if existing carbon monoxide concentrations in the atmosphere are marginal with respect to air quality standards, then specific calculations should be made for ground level concentrations of carbon monoxide. This can be referred to as microscale impact assessment. Atmospheric diffusion equations are available from many reference sources, including Turner (1969). Calculated ground level concentrations under the worst meteorological conditions should be compared to ambient air quality standards. A functional curve for microscale impact assessment is shown below (Battelle Environmental Evaluation System, 1972). The shape of the functional curve is due to the fact that carboxyhemoglobin forms in the blood at a rate which is a function of the carbon monoxide concentration. It is usually considered to be a completely reversible response, so until harmful effects occur (about 10 ppm) the functional curve is essentially flat. At toxic levels (about 40 ppm) it falls abruptly again.

Functional Curve (mesoscale)

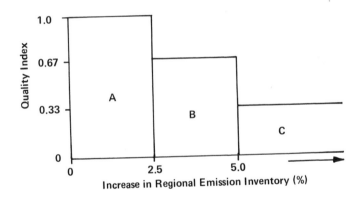

A = report mesoscale impact assessment
B = report mesoscale impact assessment, consider conducting microscale impact assessment
C = report mesoscale impact assessment, conduct microscale impact assessment.

Functional Curve (microscale)

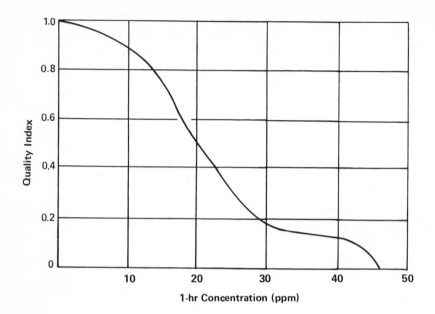

1-hr Concentration (ppm)

Remarks: Application of mesoscale concept should be based on
discussion with state air quality office. Microscale impact
assessment will probably not be necessary in most water resources projects.

Data Sources:

Air Pollutant Emission Factors (1973).
Battelle Environmental Evaluation System (1972).
Turner (1969).

References:

Canter (1977).
U.S. Department of the Army (1975).

150

ACCOUNT: ENVIRONMENTAL QUALITY

CATEGORY: AIR

SUBCATEGORY: QUALITY

VARIABLE: HYDROCARBONS

Definition and Measurement of Baseline Conditions: Hydrocarbons refer to the several types of organic compounds emitted from both man-made and natural sources. Vehicle exhausts account for over half of the complex mixture of hydrocarbons emitted to the atmosphere, with the remaining hydrocarbons occurring from natural sources such as terrestrial plants and forest vegetation. Specific components of the hydrocarbon mixture include methane, ethane, propane, and other derivatives of aliphatic and aromatic organic compounds. Hydrocarbons are of concern primarily since they can react with oxides of nitrogen to form photo-chemical oxidants (smog). Direct health effects of hydrocarbons in the atmosphere occur only at high concentrations (about 1000 ppm or more), with these levels causing interference with oxygen intake. Effects resulting from photochemical oxidant formation occur at much lower concentration levels; for example, with non-methane hydrocarbons at 200 micrograms per cubic meter ($\mu g/M^3$ or 0.30 ppm) over 3 hours (6:00 to 9:00 A.M.), photo-chemical oxidant concentrations of up to 200 $\mu g/M^3$ (0.10 ppm) can be produced some 2 to 4 hours later and persist for 1 hour. Photo-chemical oxidants at 130 $\mu g/M^3$ for an hourly average have been found to impair the performance of student athletes. The Federal ambient air quality standard for hydrocarbons is as follows:

Maximum 3-hour concentration (6-9 A.M.) not to be exceeded more than once a year = 160 $\mu g/M^3$ or 0.24 ppm.
Hydrocarbons can be measured semi-continuously through the use of gas chromatographic techniques.

Prediction of Impacts: The primary sources of hydrocarbons in relation to water resources projects are emissions from vehicular traffic, including automobiles and construction equipment. To measure this variable in the existing environment the interdisciplinary team should assemble known information on hydrocarbon concentrations in the project area, as well as summarize emission inventory data for this pollutant in the vicinity. Existing hydrocarbon concentrations can be compared with Federal and state ambient air quality standards. Prediction of impacts will involve consideration of the potential contribution of the project to the regional emission inventory for hydrocarbons. This can be called mesoscale impact assessment. Hydrocarbon emission factors for vehicles and land clearing activities can be utilized, with these being found in "Air Pollutant Emission Factors" (1973). Contributions of the potential project to the emission inventory can be expressed on a percentage basis, and the functional curve shown below can be utilized. Consideration would also need to be given to hydrocarbons which might arise from secondary growth in the project area, including population increases as well as industrial development.

If the percentage increase in the hydrocarbon emission inventory is greater than 5%, or if existing hydrocarbon concentrations in the atmosphere are marginal with respect to air quality standards, then specific calculations should be made for ground level concentrations of hydrocarbons. This can be referred to as microscale impact assessment. Atmospheric diffusion equations are available from many reference sources, including Turner (1969). Calculated ground level concentrations under the worst meteorological conditions should be compared to ambient air quality standards.

A functional curve for microscale impact assessment is shown below (Battelle Environmental Evaluation System, 1972). The shape of the functional curve is related to the degree to which the smog production potential is increased. The quality of the environment deteriorates rapidly as conditions for smog development approach (0.15 ppm to 0.25 ppm for 3-hr. average). A sharp decrease in environmental quality is shown within this range. Above the 0.25 ppm hydrocarbon concentration, the functional curve gradually levels off since the marginal impact of increases in hydrocarbon concentrations is small.

Functional Curve (mesoscale)

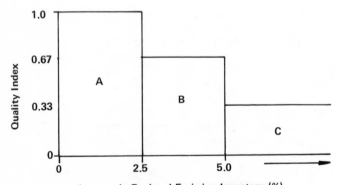

Increase in Regional Emission Inventory (%)

A = report mesoscale impact assessment
B = report mesoscale impact assessment, consider conducting
    microscale impact assessment
C = report mesoscale impact assessment, conduct microscale
    impact assessment.

152

Functional Curve (microscale)

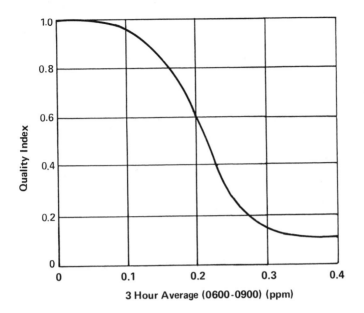

3 Hour Average (0600-0900) (ppm)

Remarks: Application of mesoscale concept should be based on discussion with state air quality office. Microscale impact assessment will probably not be necessary in most water resources projects.

Data Sources:

    Air Pollutant Emission Factors (1973).
    Battelle Environmental Evaluation System (1972).
    Turner (1969).

References:

    Canter (1977).
    U.S. Department of the Army (1975).

ACCOUNT: ENVIRONMENTAL QUALITY

CATEGORY: AIR

SUBCATEGORY: QUALITY

VARIABLE: OXIDES OF NITROGEN

Definition and Measurement of Baseline Conditions: Oxides of nitrogen, together with hydrocarbons, are the basic chemical constituents in the photo-chemical reactions leading to the formation of photochemical oxidants (smog). Many nitrogen oxide forms can be found in the atmosphere, including nitric oxide (NO), nitrogen dioxide (NO_2), and nitrous oxide (N_2O). The term oxides of nitrogen is used to represent the composite atmospheric concentration of all forms of nitrogen oxides. The primary source of oxides of nitrogen in the atmosphere is high temperature combustion of various fuels, with vehicles accounting for a major portion of all oxides of nitrogen emissions. Adverse health effects have been observed with atmospheric nitrogen oxide concentrations of 118 to 156 micrograms per cubic meter ($\mu g/M^3$), 24-hour mean over 6 months, when increases in acute bronchitis in infants and school children were noted. The Federal ambient air quality standard for oxides of nitrogen is as follows:

Annual arithmetic mean = 100 $\mu g/M^3$ or 0.05 ppm
Oxides of nitrogen can be measured through the use of a
gas absorption technique for sampling and a colorimetric
procedure for analysis.

Prediction of Impacts: The primary sources of oxides of nitrogen in relation to water resources projects are emissions from vehicular traffic, including automobiles and construction equipment. To measure this variable in the existing environment the interdisciplinary team should assemble known information on oxides of nitrogen concentrations in the project area, as well as summarize emission inventory data for this pollutant in the vicinity. Existing oxides of nitrogen concentrations can be compared with Federal and state ambient air quality standards. Prediction of impacts will involve consideration of the potential contribution of the project to the regional emission inventory for oxides of nitrogen. This can be called mesoscale impact assessment. Oxides of nitrogen emission factors for vehicles and land clearing activities can be utilized, with these being found in "Air Pollutant Emission Factors" (1973). Contributions of the potential project to the emission inventory can be expressed on a percentage basis, and the functional curve shown below can be utilized. Consideration would also need to be given to oxides of nitrogen which might arise from secondary growth in the project area, including population increases as well as industrial development.

If the percentage increase in the oxides of nitrogen emission inventory is greater than 5%, or if existing concentrations in the atmosphere are marginal with respect to air quality standards, then specific calculations should be made for ground level concentrations of oxides of nitrogen. This can be referred to as microscale impact assessment. Atmospheric diffusion equations are available from many references sources, including Turner (1969). Calculated ground level concentrations under the worst meteorological conditions should be compared to ambient air quality standards.

A functional curve for microscale impact assessment is shown below (Battelle Environmental Evaluation System, 1972). This curve is based on the fact that, generally, oxides of nitrogen concentrations below 0.05 ppm (on an annual average basis) do not pose a health problem. Exposure above this concentration can be correlated with a higher incidence of acute respiratory problems. At levels higher than those normally present in the ambient air (about 0.05 ppm), nitrogen oxides can act as a toxic agent and the functional curve reflects a decrease in environmental quality.

Functional Curve (mesoscale)

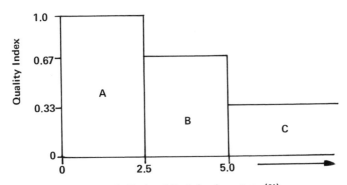

Increase in Regional Emission Inventory (%)

A = report mesoscale impact assessment
B = report mesoscale impact assessment, consider conducting microscale impact assessment
C = report mesoscale impact assessment, conduct microscale impact assessment.

Functional Curve (microscale)

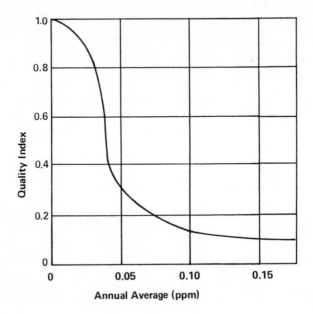

Annual Average (ppm)

Remarks: Application of mesoscale concept should be based on discussion with state air quality office. Microscale impact assessment will probably not be necessary in most water resources projects.

Data Sources:

    Air Pollutant Emission Factors (1973).
    Battelle Environmental Evaluation System (1972).
    Turner (1969).

References:

    Canter (1977).
    U.S. Department of the Army (1975).

ACCOUNT: ENVIRONMENTAL QUALITY

CATEGORY: AIR

SUBCATEGORY: QUALITY

VARIABLE: PARTICULATES

Definition and Measurement of Baseline Conditions: Particulates are finely divided solid and liquid particles suspended
in ambient air. They range from 0.01 microns to over 100
microns in diameter. Particulates can occur in the atmosphere
as a result of both natural and man-made sources. Natural
wind-blown dust provides a "background" particulate concentration, with man-made sources including various construction
activities and industrial processes. Adverse health effects
resulting from particulates in the atmosphere have been
observed for annual mean concentrations of 80 micrograms per
cubic meter ($\mu g/M^3$). Particulates may aggravate bronchitis,
emphysema, and cardiovascular diseases. Particulates soil
clothes and buildings, and can cause serious visibility problems. Steel and other metal structures can be corroded as a
result of exposure to particulates and humidity. The Federal
ambient air quality standards for particulates are as follows:

Primary standards protective for public health
Annual geometric mean = 75 $\mu g/M^3$
Maximum 24-hr. concentration not to be exceeded more
than once per year = 260 $\mu g/M^3$.

Secondary standards protective for public welfare
Annual geometric mean = 40 $\mu g/M^3$
Maximum 24-hr. concentration not to be exceeded more
than once per year = 15 $\mu g/M^3$

Total suspended particulates can be measured via a high-
volume sampler and gravimetric analysis of the fil-
tered materials.

Prediction of Impacts: The primary sources of particulates in
relation to water resources projects are emissions from land
clearing and other construction activities. To measure this
variable in the existing environment the interdisciplinary
team should assemble known information on particulate concentrations in the project area, as well as summarize emission inventory data for this pollutant in the vicinity. Existing particulate concentrations can be compared with Federal and state
ambient air quality standards. Prediction of impacts will
involve consideration of the potential contribution of the
project to the regional emission inventory for particulates.

157

This can be called mesoscale impact assessment. Particulate emission factors for land clearing and other construction activities can be utilized, with these being found in "Air Pollution Emission Factors" (1973). Contributions of the potential project to the emission inventory can be expressed on a percentage basis, and the functional curve shown below can be utilized. Consideration would also need to be given to particulates which might arise from secondary growth in the project area, including population increases as well as industrial development.

If the percentage increase in the particulate emission inventory is greater than 5%, or if existing particulate concentrations in the atmosphere are marginal with respect to air quality standards, then specific calculations should be made for ground level concentrations of particulates. This can be referred to as microscale impact assessment. Atmospheric diffusion equations are available from many reference sources, including Turner (1969). Calculated ground level concentrations under the worst meteorological conditions should be compared to ambient air quality standards. The functional curve shown below for microscale impact assessment is based on the fact that the effects of particulates on environmental quality range from visibility problems to health impairments (Battelle Environmental Evaluation System, 1972). Visibility decreases occur at concentrations as low as 25 $\mu g/M^3$. As the concentration of particulates increases to about 200 $\mu g/M^3$, human health begins to be affected. These concentration levels refer to 24-hour mean values. Particulate concentrations of less than 25 $\mu g/M^3$ are considered less desirable for the environment since they provide condensation nuclei upon which fog and cloud droplets settle.

Functional Curve (mesoscale)

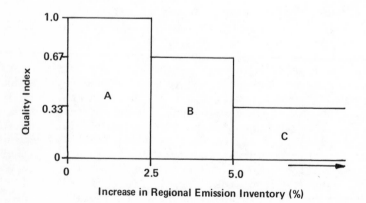

A = report mesoscale impact assessment
B = report mesoscale impact assessment, consider conduc-
    ting microscale impact assessment
C = report mesoscale impact assessment, conduct microscale
    impact assessment.

Functional Curve (microscale)

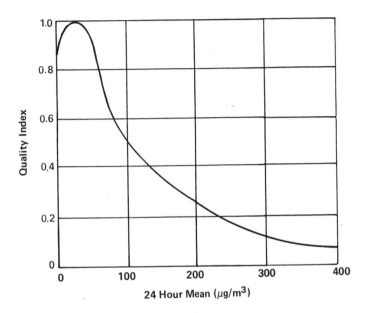

Remarks: Application of mesoscale concept should be based on
discussion with state air quality office, Microscale impact
assessment may be necessary during the construction phase of
water resources projects.

Data Sources:

    Air Pollutant Emission Factors (1973).
    Battelle Environmental Evaluation System (1972).
    Turner (1969).

References:

    Canter (1977).
    U.S. Department of the Army (1975).

ACCOUNT: ENVIRONMENTAL QUALITY

CATEGORY: AIR

SUBCATEGORY: CLIMATOLOGY

VARIABLE: DIFFUSION FACTOR

Definition and Measurement of Baseline Conditions: Diffusion
factor is a general term used to describe the atmospheric dispersion potential for an area. A parameter which can serve
as an indicator of diffusion/dispersion capability is episode-
days. An episode-day can be defined according to mixing height,
average wind speed in the mixer layer, degree of precipitation,
and time period of persistence. Holzworth (1972) provides
extensive information on episode-days in the United States.
The attached figure shows isopleths of the total number of
episode-days in five years with mixing heights equal to or
less than 500 meters, wind speeds equal to or less than 4
meters per second, and no significant precipitation for at
least two days.

Prediction of Impacts: Measurement of this variable would
involve use of the attached figure showing episode-days. An
approximation should be made of the number of episode-days
occurring in the general vicinity of the potential project
site over a five-year period. Prediction of the impacts of a
potential project on the number of episode-days would involve
qualitative consideration of whether or not potential climato-
logical changes such as increases in relative humidity would
cause the meteorological conditions to be changed sufficiently
to increase the number of episode-days (lower the atmospheric
dispersion potential). However, despite the lack of finite
knowledge on microclimatological impacts, it appears unlikely
that water resources projects could cause changes in the number
of episode-days in an area.

Functional Curve

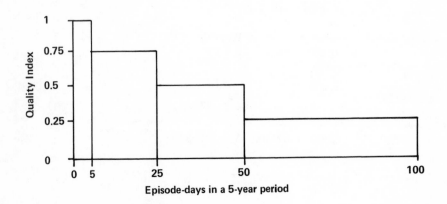

160

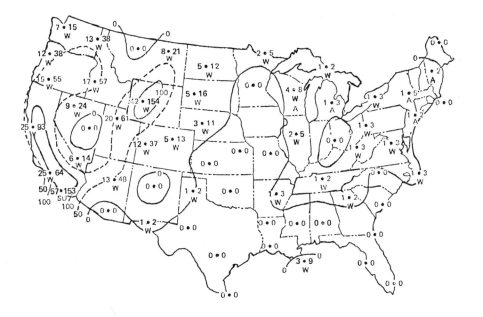

Isoplaths of total number of episode-days in 5 yr with mixing
heights ≤500 m, wind speeds ≤4 m/sec, and no significant precipitation for episodes lasting at least 2 days. Numerals on
left and right give total number of episodes and episode-days,
respectively. Season with greatest number of episode-days indicated as W (winter), SP (spring), SU (summer) or A (autumn).

Remarks: This variable is of greatest potential use in terms
of general site selection, however, available finite information at various potential sites may be lacking, thus a high
degree of resolution cannot be achieved.

Data Sources:

   Holzworth (1972).

References:

   Canter (1977).

HUMAN INTERFACE VARIABLES

CATEGORY: HUMAN INTERFACE

SUBCATEGORY: NOISE

VARIABLE: NOISE

Definition and Measurement of Baseline Conditions: Noise can be defined as unwanted sound or sound in the wrong place at the wrong time. The aspect of being unwanted implies that it has an adverse effect on human beings in their environment, including land, structures, and domestic animals. Noise can also disturb natural wildlife and ecological systems. Noise measurements are expressed by the term "sound pressure level" (SPL), which is the logarithmic ratio of the sound pressure to a reference pressure, and is expressed as a dimensionless unit of power, the decibel (dB). The reference pressure level is 0.0002 microbars. The attached table shows various sound pressure levels associated with recognized sources of noise. Noise levels in a given area can be determined through the use of a sound level meter.

Prediction of Impacts: Existing noise levels within the project area should be established by conduction of noise monitoring surveys or determination of land uses in the vicinity. If land usage is used to estimate existing noise level, then general reference sources such as Canter (1977) which relate land usage and noise should be utilized. Prediction of impacts for a potential project should include consideration of both construction phase and operational phase noise generation. Construction phase noise levels are shown in EPA (1972). Operational phase noise may occur from usage of the water resources project as well as from secondary development, including population increases and industrial development. Specific noise levels from man's activities are found in many reference sources, including EPA (1972). Prediction of the anticipated noise levels at various distances from the source can be estimated through the use of either a point source propagation model or a line source propagation model. Specific information relative to these calculations is contained in Canter (1977).
    Once existing noise levels, as well as the anticipated noise levels resulting from project construction and operation are known for an area, they can be subjected to assessment based on the functional curve shown below (Battelle Environmental Evaluation System, 1972). This functional curve is based on two indicators of noise, intensity (expressed as decibels on the A scale -- the A scale refers to the scale of noise measurement which most closely resembles the response of the human ear to noise), and frequency of occurrence and distribution within the project area. Specific data could be utilized to establish

the intensity, while qualitative judgment would have to be exercised by the interdisciplinary team in defining frequency of occurrence and distribution within the project area. In general, the greater the intensity and frequency of occurrence, the lower the environmental quality. In some locations it might be appropriate to compare existing and predicted noise levels to established noise standards and criteria. There are no Federal standards on noise, although criteria have been published by the Environmental Protection Agency (1974).

Functional Curve (Battelle Environmental Evaluation System, 1972):

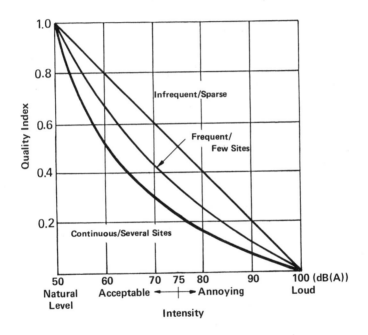

SPL, Sound Pressure, and Recognized Sources of
Noise in Our Daily Experiences

Sound pressure, μbar	SPL, dBA	Example
0.0002	0	Threshold of hearing
0.00063	10	
0.002	20	Studio for sound pictures
0.0063	30	Studio for speech broadcasting
0.02	40	Very quiet room
0.063	50	Residence
0.2	60	Conventional speech
0.63	70	Street traffic at 100 ft
1.0	74	Passing automobile at 20 ft
2.0	80	Light trucks at 20 ft
6.3	90	Subway at 20 ft
20	100	Looms in textile mill
63	110	Loud motorcycle at 20 ft
200	120	Peak level from rock and roll band
2,000	140	Jet plane on the ground at 20 ft

Remarks: Considerable professional judgment will be required
in assembling and interpreting noise information. Noise
specialists may be required in urban water resources projects.

Data Sources:

Canter (1977).
Environmental Protection Agency (1972).
Environmental Protection Agency (1974).
Battelle Environmental Evaluation System (1972).

References:

Chanlett (1973).

ACCOUNT: ENVIRONMENTAL QUALITY

CATEGORY: HUMAN INTERFACE

SUBCATEGORY: ESTHETICS/TERRESTRIAL

VARIABLE: WIDTH AND ALIGNMENT

Definition and Measurement of Baseline Conditions: The proportion of the width of a canyon or gorge to its depth (measured from the highest surrounding points to the valley floor) and the deviation of a watercourse from a straight line have a direct bearing on the esthetic quality of a deep valley or stream. A valley has its greatest esthetic value if its width is nearly equal to its depth, less so if its width is two or more times its depth. A stream or long and narrow reservoir is esthetically most pleasing if its path is tortuous, less so if it is gently meandering, and least of all if it approaches a straight line.

In order to measure this variable the interdisciplinary team would need to visit the project site and develop general estimates of the width of the valley location relative to the depth (distance from high surrounding points to the valley floor). The interdisciplinary team would also have to qualitatively determine the extent of watercourse deviation from a straight line.

Prediction of Impacts: Prediction of the impact of a potential project on these factors would include a determination of changes in width and alignment. It is unlikely that any changes in terms of valley width to depth would be accomplished by a water resources project. More likely changes would be associated with inundation, with converting a tortuous stream to a meandering stream, or a meandering stream to a straight stream. Qualitative judgment would have to be exercised by the interdisciplinary team in order to estimate changes in stream alignment without a project as well as with a project.

<u>Functional Curve</u> (Battelle Environmental Evaluation System, 1972).

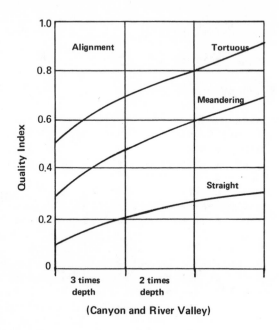

(Canyon and River Valley)

<u>Remarks</u>:   The professional judgment of a recreation specialist would be valuable for this variable.

<u>Data Sources</u>:

Battelle Environmental Evaluation System (1972).

<u>References</u>:

Leopold (1969).

ACCOUNT: ENVIRONMENTAL QUALITY

CATEGORY: HUMAN INTERFACE

SUBCATEGORY: ESTHETICS/TERRESTRIAL

VARIABLE: VARIETY WITHIN VEGETATION TYPES

Definition and Measurement of Baseline Conditions: The greater the variety among species of plants with a vegetation type, the more visually appealing a site is likely to be. For example, a mixed forest of both deciduous and coniferous trees is usually more colorful and esthetically interesting than a forest consisting of only one or the other. Additionally, attractive and unusual species of plants greatly enhance the esthetic interest and appeal of an area.

Determination of the baseline conditions for this variable would involve a site visit to the potential project area by the interdisciplinary team. The participation of a botanist would be desirable. Qualitative judgment would have to be exercised as to the extent of variety among vegetation types. In general, the greater the plant variety, the greater the environmental quality.

Prediction of Impacts: Impact prediction would involve qualitative judgment as to the areal extent of changes in plant varieties within the project area. Consideration should be given to natural seasonal changes as well as ecological succession when evaluating this variable.

<u>Functional Curve</u> (Battelle Environmental Evaluation System, 1972):

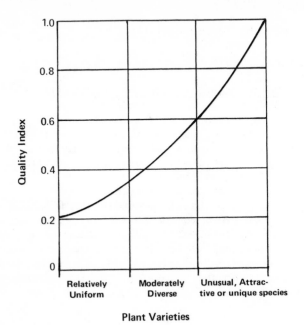

Plant Varieties

<u>Remarks</u>: The **professional expertise** of a botanist would be required to properly consider and assess this variable.

<u>Data Sources</u>:

Battelle Environmental Evaluation System (1972).

<u>References</u>:

None.

ACCOUNT: ENVIRONMENTAL QUALITY

CATEGORY: HUMAN INTERFACE

SUBCATEGORY: ESTHETICS/TERRESTRIAL

VARIABLE: ANIMALS - DOMESTIC

Definition and Measurement of Baseline Conditions: Domestic animals in a pastoral setting, particularly cattle and horses, are an asset to the esthetics of a landscape. Such animals give scale, movement, and life to a rural composition, but their overabundance adds little to a scene's visual quality, and may, because of over-grazing or odor, detract from it. For this reason the functional curve given below decreases in environmental quality as the abundance increases.

Measurement of this variable would involve a site visit to the potential project area by the interdisciplinary team. The participation of a zoologist would be desirable. Qualitative judgment relative to the number of domestic animals occupying the landscape would be necessary in order to decide if they are scarce, common, or abundant. Consideration would need to be given to seasonal variations in the number of domestic animals occupying the landscape.

Prediction of Impacts: Prediction of the impact of a project would include consideration of the amount of the landscape which would be lost to grazing. Qualitative judgment would have to be exercised in estimating the potential change in number of domestic animals occupying the landscape.

<u>Functional Curve</u> (Battelle Environmental Evaluation System, 1972):

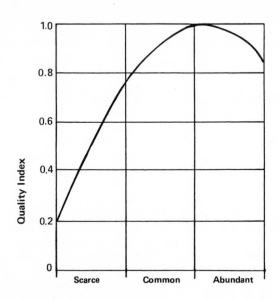

<u>Remarks</u>: The professional expertise of a zoologist would be required to properly consider and assess this variable.

<u>Data Sources</u>:

Battelle Environmental Evaluation System (1972).

<u>References</u>:

None.

ACCOUNT: ENVIRONMENTAL QUALITY

CATEGORY: HUMAN INTERFACE

SUBCATEGORY: ESTHETICS/TERRESTRIAL

VARIABLE: NATIVE FAUNA

Definition and Measurement of Baseline Conditions: The presence
of wild mammals and birds in an area has an esthetic value.
Large herbivorous mammals (moose, elk, deer, antelope, mountain
goats and sheep) and smaller mammals and all wild birds contribute to the esthetic value of an area's sights and sounds.
Large carnivorous animals might have mixed esthetic values.
For example, people thrill at the sight of a grizzly bear, but
it is possible that their fear might curtail their activity and
reduce their overall enjoyment of an area.   The presence of
threatened or endangered species - California condor, bald
eagle, mountain lion, or trumpeter swan, for example - is a
prime esthetic asset and would doubtless provide the incentive
for countless visitations to a site.   Generally, the small,
cold-blooded vertebrates are also esthetically pleasing ele-
ments of the water and land composition.   Fish, particularly
game fish, frogs and tadpoles, turtles, and lizards add movement and natural interest.   Some reptiles may have mixed esthetic values.   For example, though many people enjoy sighting
and identifying all wildlife, including poisonous snakes,
alligators, and the single species of poisonous lizards, pre-
cautions taken against the dangers of these animals may detract
from visitors' enjoyment of a site.   Although not considered
as a part of this variable, invertebrates such as butterflies,
dragonflies and bees also have a positive effect on the esthetic quality of an area.
    Measurement of this variable would involve a site visit
to the potential project area by an interdisciplinary team.
The participation of a zoologist is required.   Published information on native fauna in the area, when coupled with qualitative judgments developed from the site visit, will enable the
interdisciplinary team to estimate the relative abundance of
both small and large native animals.

Prediction of Impacts: Prediction of the impact of a potential project on the native fauna in an area will involve consideration of the areal extent of land use changes and qualitative judgment as to the impacts of these changes on the relative abundance of both small and large native animals.   Consideration should be given to the impacts of secondary land
development that would possibly occur as a result of the construction and operation of a particular project.

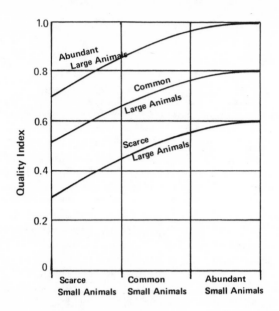

Remarks: The professional expertise of a zoologist would be required to properly consider and assess this variable.

Data Sources:

Battelle Environmental Evaluation System (1972).

References:

None.

ACCOUNT: ENVIRONMENTAL QUALITY

CATEGORY: HUMAN INTERFACE

SUBCATEGORY: ESTHETICS/AQUATIC

VARIABLE: APPEARANCE OF WATER

Definition and Measurement of Baseline Conditions: The esthetic
quality of water depends on its clarity and flow characteristics. Pure, clear water is most desirable; fast water is considered more visually appealing than slow or static water.
Fast flow can do little to offset the esthetic drawbacks of
turbidity or color. Silt, sediment, and algae can decrease the
visual quality of water.

   Measurement of this variable would require a visit to the
potential project site by the interdisciplinary team. In fact,
visits should be made on several occasions in order to ascertain seasonal differences in flow characteristics and clarity.
Following the seasonally related site visits, the interdisciplinary team should qualitatively decide if the flow characteristics are static, slow, moderate, or characterized by white
water. In addition, a qualitative decision would have to be
made regarding whether the water was generally clear, moderately
turbid, or turbid.

Prediction of Impacts: Prediction of the impact of a project
would involve the exercise of qualitative judgment by the
interdisciplinary team in estimating whether the flow characteristics would change as a result of the project, as well as the
extent of change in water clarity. Consideration should be
given to potential changes during both construction and operational phases.

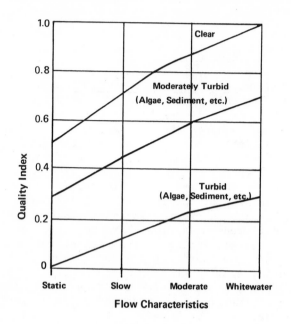

Remarks: Persons trained as recreation specialists can aid in
the assemblage and interpretation of information on this
variable.

Data Sources:

    Battelle Environmental Evaluation System (1972).

References:

    Leopold (1969).

ACCOUNT: ENVIRONMENTAL QUALITY

CATEGORY: HUMAN INTERFACE

SUBCATEGORY: ESTHETICS/AQUATIC

VARIABLE: ODOR AND FLOATING MATERIALS

Definition and Measurement of Baseline Conditions: Water that
gives off an unpleasant odor or that carries excessive quantities of floating debris, oil, or scum is esthetically dis-
pleasing. It is recognized that certain mild, natural water
odors, even though noticeable, are not always disagreeable and
should be rated only slightly lower than no odor at all.

Measurement of this variable would require several
seasonally-related site visits to the potential project area
by the interdisciplinary team. Estimates would need to be
made regarding the extent of detached floating materials in
the existing water body, as well as any odors resulting from
floating materials, oil, or scum. Qualitative judgment would
be necessary to determine if detached floating materials could
be categorized as light, moderate, heavy, or non-existent (none).
Qualitative judgment would also be required to classify odors
as to whether they are disagreeable, noticeable, or lacking.

Prediction of Impacts: Prediction of the impacts of a potential project would require qualitative judgment relative to
whether future conditions would be characterized by floating
materials and odors. Consideration would need to be given as
to whether or not the potential project would potentiate floating materials and odors, or encourage the development of
upstream control measures to eliminate the concerns. Consideration should also be given to the construction phase of the
project as well as subsequent planned uses of the water
resource.

<u>Functional Curve</u> (Battelle Environmental Evaluation System, 1972).

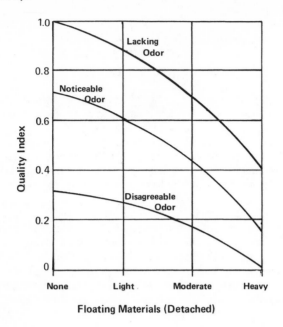

Floating Materials (Detached)

<u>Remarks</u>: Persons trained as recreation specialists can aid in the assemblage and interpretation of information on this variable.

<u>Data Sources</u>:

Battelle Environmental Evaluation System (1972).

<u>References</u>:

Leopold (1969).

ACCOUNT: ENVIRONMENTAL QUALITY

CATEGORY: HUMAN INTERFACE

SUBCATEGORY: ESTHETICS/AIR

VARIABLE: ODOR AND VISUAL QUALITY

Definition and Measurement of Baseline Conditions: Polluted
air is esthetically offensive in at least two ways: (1) it
may carry disagreeable odors and (2) it may contain visible
gases or suspended particles which render the vista dull and
flat, or even practically invisible. The odor and visual quality parameter is rated very low if a disagreeable odor is present, while a lack of odor or a pleasant odor rates highest.
The scent of evergreens, wildflowers, or wild herbs is a
delightful asset to the esthetic quality of a site. Frequent
view-obscuring haze, dust or smog has a low rating while con-
sistently crystal-clear air rates highest. Clean, bright air
is increasingly sought after by town and city dwellers in their
outdoor recreational and esthetic experiences as an end in
itself, and so is very important in any visual considerations.
    Measurement of this variable would include the assemblage
of existing information relative to air quality in the potential project area. In addition, site visits on several occasions should be made by the interdisciplinary team to ascertain
the visual quality of the area and the potential presence of
disagreeable odors. Qualitative judgment would have to be
utilized in categorizing visual quality relative to whether it
is heavy and frequent, moderate and occasional, or clear. The
odor characteristics of the air would also need to be categorized relative to the presence of disagreeable odors, lacking
in odors, or the occurrence of pleasant odors.

Prediction of Impacts: Prediction of the impact of a potential
project should involve consideration of both construction and
operational phases. Particular attention would need to be
given to secondary impacts created by population increases,
and potential industrial development within the area.

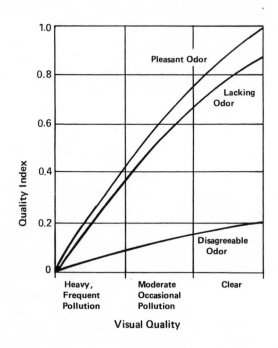

Remarks: The expertise of a recreation specialist would be valuable in the assemblage and interpretation of information.

Data Sources:

Battelle Environmental Evaluation System (1972).

References:

Leopold (1969).

ACCOUNT: ENVIRONMENTAL QUALITY

CATEGORY: HUMAN INTERFACE

SUBCATEGORY: ESTHETICS/NOISE

VARIABLE: SOUND

Definition and Measurement of Baseline Conditions: Sounds are
rated according to their pleasantness or unpleasantness, and
their frequency. Pleasant sounds include natural animal sounds
like the songs of birds, the peeps and croaks of frogs, and
the clarion calls of wild geese. Other pleasant sounds might
be produced by the wind as it rushes through evergreen trees
or whistles through rock formations, and by water as it splashes
over rocks or laps against a shore. Unpleasant sounds include
the loud, discordant, and unnatural noises produced by indus-
try, highway vehicles, airplanes, and other machines. These
clash with the peace and solitude of nature, thus robbing
recreationists of the very experience they may be seeking.
    Measurement of this variable would require a site visit
by the interdisciplinary team in order to estimate the sound
frequency in the potential project area. Two levels of occurrence (frequent and occasional) should be used along with two
levels of human perceptiveness of sound (unpleasant and pleasant). Qualitative judgment regarding the sounds which charac-
terize the potential project area would be required.

Prediction of Impacts: Prediction of the impact of a project
shall include consideration of sounds from both the construction and operations phases. Again, qualitative judgment would
be required relative to the sound occurrence and human perceptiveness.

Functional Curve (Battelle Environmental Evaluation System, 1972).

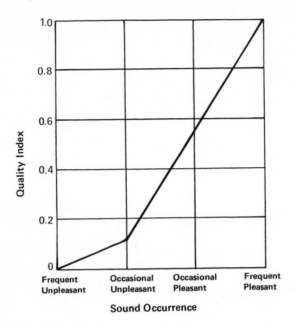

Remarks: The expertise of a recreation specialist would be valuable in the assemblage and interpretation of information.

Data Sources:

Battelle Environmental Evaluation System (1972).

References:

Battelle Dredging Impact Assessment Method (1974).
Leopold (1969).

ACCOUNT: ENVIRONMENTAL QUALITY

CATEGORY: HUMAN INTERFACE

SUBCATEGORY: HISTORICAL

VARIABLE: HISTORICAL INTERNAL AND EXTERNAL PACKAGES

Definition and Measurement of Baseline Conditions: Historical
sites within the United States have become increasingly important within this century relative to their historic value,
esthetic quality, and cultural significance. Places of historic
value are those which have been the location of events of significant importance in the history of the United States.
Things having historic value can be sites, objects, or structures.
    The concept of a "package" refers to the fact that every-
thing of historic interest that occurs in an area is thought
of as one "package." Each occurrence, in and of itself, is
not given a "with-without" evaluation. The "package" itself
is given a "with-without" evaluation. The procedure of identifying parameters that are relevant to a particular project
evaluation involves the following steps for each individual
parameter:

(1) Identify all occurrences within the project area
     that apply to this parameter.
(2) Think of all the occurrences totally as a package.
(3) Determine whether or not this total "package" is of
     any significance.
(4) (a) If it is determined that the package does have
          significance, refer to the functional curve to
          make a "with-without" evaluation of the package.
     (b) If it is determined that the package does not
          have significance, it will not be included in
          the evaluation.

    In steps (3) and (4), the word "significance" is of utmost
importance to the evaluation procedure and the proper use of
the functional curve. Two more concepts are used to clarify
the meaning of significance. These are the terms "internal"
and "external." These terms help to identify the people to
whom the package has significance. "Internal" refers to people
who have been identified in the proposed project plan as being
somehow affected by the proposed project - either beneficially
or adversely - in one or more of its sectors. Thus, a package
of "internal significance" refers to a package of occurrences
of historical interest to those people who are being directly
affected by the proposed project. "External" refers to all
other people outside of the project area who may have an interest in the effects or impacts caused by the proposed project.

183

These two terms do not necessarily have a particular geographical connotation or boundary, although in some projects they
may.

Measurement of this variable would involve assemblage of
known information regarding historic resources in the potential
project area. Reference sources include the National Register
of Historic Places, State Historic Preservation Officers, and
state and local historical commissions/societies. Historical
resources previously included on the National Register, as well
as those eligible for potential inclusion, should be identified.
In order to assess the importance of the historical package,
the interdisciplinary team should identify local people who
would be somehow affected by the proposed project - either
beneficially or adversely - and discuss with them their assessment of the significance of the historical resources in the
area. Persons outside the project area should also be queried.

Therefore, before a functional curve can be used, the
question must be asked - "Do the occurrences identified as
being a part of this package have significance only to people
in the project area, or do they have significance to people
outside of the project area?" If the answer to the first part
of the question is yes, then the package is an "internal package" and the appropriate functional curve is applied. If the
second part of the question is answered by yes, the package
is considered an "external package" and the appropriate functional curve should be used. If the package has aspects of
both internal and external significance, it should be considered an "external package."

The bases for determing the value (High, High-Medium,
Low-Medium, and Low) of the package are:

(1) The number of people visiting or using the components
     of the package;
(2) The intensity of interest shown by those people
     making use of it;
(3) The intensity of objections expressed by people if
     change to the package or a part of the package is
     indicated;
(4) The value placed on the package by an expert in the
     field (historian).

Prediction of Impacts: Prediction of the impact of a project
would include consideration of the possible losses of historical resources as a result of project construction and operation.
Consideration should be given to the impacts of potential secondary development. Qualitative judgment would have to be
exercised by the interdisciplinary team in ascertaining the
value significance of the resultant historical internal or
external package following project initiation.

The external package functional curve shown below was
designed in such a way as to give more value to a package that

has "external" significance (Battelle Environmental Evaluation System, 1972). This was done because it was felt that external significance indicated that something was of more importance to more people; therefore, it should have more value. The quality descriptors used for the external package value function are the same as for the internal package value function, i.e., High, High-Medium, Low-Medium, Low, and None. The terms are the same, but their value is higher. The descriptor "none" is used to identify a package which no longer has significance or value either because it no longer exists (e.g., inundation by the reservoir) or because of a high degree of adverse effects caused by a "with" situation.

Functional Curve - Internal Package

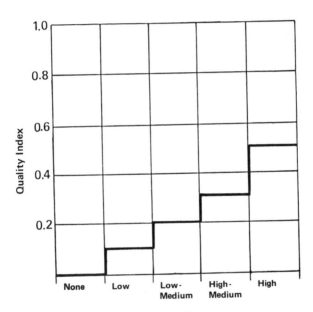

Value Significance

Functional Curve - External Package

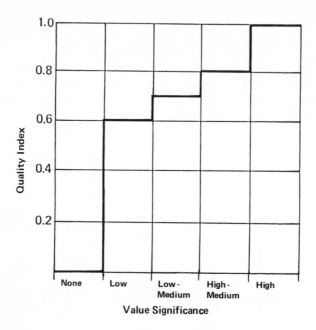

Remarks: A professional historian may be necessary for proper assemblage and interpretation of information.

Data Sources:

Battelle Environmental Evaluation System (1972).

References:

McGimsey (1973).

ACCOUNT: ENVIRONMENTAL QUALITY

CATEGORY: HUMAN INTERFACE

SUBCATEGORY: ARCHAEOLOGICAL

VARIABLE: ARCHAEOLOGICAL INTERNAL AND EXTERNAL PACKAGES

Definition and Measurement of Baseline Conditions: Archaeological resources within the United States have become increasingly important within the last decade. With the passage of
the National Environmental Policy Act in 1969, greater attention was placed on the preservation of various cultural resources, including archaeological resources. Archaeological
resources can be defined as objects and areas made or modified
by humans, as well as the data associated with these artifacts
and features. Objects include such artifacts as Indian arrow-
heads, stone axes, and broken or whole pottery vessels. Areas
made or modified by humans include hunting stations, temporary
camps, permanent settlements, and habitation sites.

The concept of a "package" refers to the fact that every-
thing of archeological interest that occurs in an area is
thought of as one "package." Each occurrence, in and of itself,
is not given a "with-without" evaluation. The "package" itself
is given a "with-without" evaluation. The procedure of identifying parameters that are relevant to a particular project
evaluation involves the following steps for each individual
parameter:

(1) Identify all occurrences within the project area
    that apply to this parameter.
(2) Think of all the occurrences totally as a package.
(3) Determine whether or not this total "package" is of
    any significance.
(4) (a) If it is determined that the package does have
        significance, refer to the functional curve to
        make a "with-without" evaluation of the package.
    (b) If it is determined that the package does not
        have significance, it will not be included in
        the evaluation.

In steps (3) and (4), the word "significance" is of utmost
importance to the evaluation procedure and the proper use of
the functional curve. Two more concepts are used to clarify
the meaning of isgnificance. These are the terms "internal"
and "external." These terms help to identify the people to
whom the package has significance. "Internal" refers to people
who have been identified in the proposed project plan as being
somehow affected by the proposed project - either beneficially
or adversely - in one or more of its sectors. Thus, a package
of "internal significance" refers to a package of occurrences

of archeological interest to those people who are being directly affected by the proposed project. "External" refers to all other people outside of the project area who may have an interest in the effects or impacts caused by the proposed project. These two terms do not necessarily have a particular geographical connotation or boundary, although in some projects they may.

Measurement of this variable would involve the assemblage of known information on the archaeological resources in the project area, as well as the potential for additional archaeological resources being in the area but as yet not discovered. The expertise of a professional archaeologist would be required in order for the interdisciplinary team to measure this variable. In addition, persons living within and outside the project area should be interviewed with regard to their perceptions of the significance of the archaeological resources. Qualitative judgment on the part of the interdisciplinary team, coupled with the professional judgment of a professional archaeologist, should be utilized to determine the value significance of the archaelogical packages.

Therefore, before a functional curve can be used, the question must be asked - "Do the occurrences identified as being a part of this package have significance only to people in the project area, or do they have significance to people outside of the project area?" If the answer to the first part of the question is yes, then the package is an "internal package" and the appropriate functional curve is applied. If the second part of the question is answered by yes, the package is considered an "external package" and the appropriate functional curve should be used. If the package has aspects of both internal and external significance, it should be considered an "external package."

The bases for determining the value (High, High-Medium, Low-Medium, and Low) of the package are:

(1) The number of people visiting or using the components of the package;

(2) The intensity of interest shown by those people making use of it;

(3) The intensity of objections expressed by people if change to the package or a part of the package is indicated;

(4) The value placed on the package by an expert in the field (archaeologist).

Prediction of Impacts: Prediction of impacts would include consideration of the possible effects of project construction and operation on the archaeological resources in the area. Consideration should be given to the possible consequences of secondary development. Qualitative judgment would again have to be exercised by the interdisciplinary team and a professional archaeologist in estimating the value significance of the resultant archaeological resources in the project area.

The external package functional curve shown below was designed in such a way as to give more value to a package that has "external" significance (Battelle Environmental Evaluation System, 1972). This was done because it was felt that external significance indicated that something was of more importance to more people; therefore, should have more value. The quality descriptors used for the external package value function are the same as for the internal package value function, i.e., High, High-Medium, Low-Medium, Low, and None. The terms are the same, but their value is higher. The descriptor "None" is used to identify a package which no longer has significance or value either because it no longer exists (e.g., inundation by the reservoir) or because of a high degree of adverse effects caused by a "with" situation.

Functional Curve - Internal Package

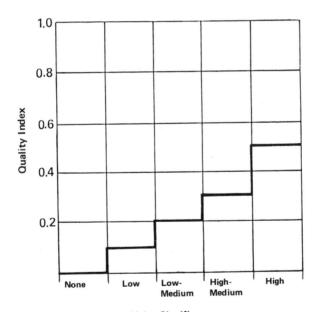

Value Significance

Functional Curve - External Package

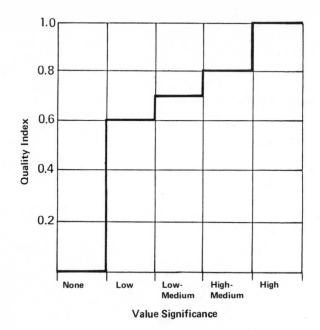

Value Significance

Remarks: A professional archaeologist will be necessary for proper assemblage and interpretation of information.

Data Sources:

Battelle Environmental Evaluation System (1972).

References:

McGimsey (1973).

SELECTED REFERENCES

"Battelle Dredging Impact Assessment Method," 1974, draft report
prepared by Battelle-Columbus Laboratories, Columbus, Ohio,
for U.S. Army Engineer Waterways Experiment Station, CE,
Vicksburg, Miss.

"Battelle Environmental Evaluation System for Water Resource
Planning," 1972, report submitted to U.S. Bureau of
Reclamation, by Dee, N., et al., Battelle-Columbus Labora-
tories, Columbus, Ohio.

"Battelle Water Resource Project," 1974, report submitted to
U.S. Environmental Protection Agency, by Warner, M. L., et
al., entitled "An Assessment Methodology for the Environmental Impacts of Water Resources Projects," EPA-600/5-74-016,
Battelle-Columbus Laboratories, Columbus, Ohio.

Bechtel, T. J. and Copeland, B. J., 1970, "Fish Species Diversity
Indices as Indicators of Pollution in Galveston Bay, Texas,"
Contr. Mar. Sci., Univ. Texas, Austin, Texas 15: 103-132.

Bell, D. T. and Johnson, F. J., 1974, "Flood-Caused Tree
Mortality around Illinois Reservoirs," Trans. Ill. State
Acad. Sci. 67: 28-37.

Brookhaven Symposium in Biology, 1969, "Diversity and Stability
in Ecological Systems," Number 22, Brookhaven, Washington.

Bureau of Reclamation, 1972, "Guidelines for Implementing
Principles and Standards for Multi-objective Planning of
Water Resources," Washington, D.C.

Canter, L. W., 1977, Environmental Impact Assessment, McGraw-
Hill Book Company, New York, NY.

Chanlett, E. T., 1973, Environmental Protection, McGraw-Hill
Book Company, New York, NY.

Collier, B. D., et al., 1973, Dynamic Ecology, Prentice-Hall,
Inc., Englewood Cliffs, NJ.

Dayton, P. K., 1975, "Experimental Evaluation of Ecological
Dominance in a Rocky Intertidal Algal Community," Ecological
Monographs, 45: 137-159.

191

Environmental Impact Center, Inc., 1973, "A Methodology for Assessing Environmental Impact of Water Resources Development," prepared by Environmental Impact Center, Inc., Cambridge, Mass., for U.S. Department of Interior, Office of Water Resources Research, Washington, D.C.

Environmental Protection Agency, 1972, "Report to the President and Congress on Noise," 92nd Cong., 2nd Sess., Document 92-63, Washington, D.C.

Environmental Protection Agency, 1973, "Air Pollution Emission Factors," Publ. AP 42, Research Triangle Park, N.C.

Environmental Protection Agency, 1973, Methods for Identifying the Nature and Extent of Non-Point Sources of Pollutants," Publ. EPA-430/9-73-014, Washington, D.C.

Environmental Protection Agency, 1974, "Information of Levels of Environmental Noise Requisite to Protect Public Health and Welfare with an Adequate Margin of Safety," Publ. 550/9-74-004, Washington, D.C.

Glasgow, L. L. and Noble, R. E., 1971, "The Importance of Bottomland Hadrwoods to Wildlife," Proc. First Symp. on Southeastern Hardwoods, U.S. Forest Service, Atlanta, Ga. pp. 30-43.

Heady, H. F., 1975, Rangeland Management, McGraw-Hill Book Company, New York, N.Y.

Holzworth, G. C., 1972, "Mixing Heights, Wind Speeds, and Potential for Urban Air Pollution Throughout the Contiguous United States," Publ. AP-101, Environmental Protection Agency, Research Triangle Park, N.C.

Hooper, G., Crawford, S and Harlow, F., 1973, "Bird Density and Diversity as Related to Vegetation in Forest Recreational Areas," Jour. of Forestry, Vol. 12, p. 71.

Horn, H. S., 1974, "The Ecology Succession," Ann Rev. Ecological Systems, 5: 25-38.

Hosner, J. F. and Minckler, L. S., 1963, "Bottomland Hardwood Forests of Southern Illinois--Regeneration and Succession," Ecology 44(1): 29-41.

Hynes, H. B. N., 1970, The Ecology of Running Waters, Univ. of Toronto Press, Toronto, Canada.

Jenkins, M., 1968, "The Influence of Some Environmental Factors on Standing Crop and Harvest of Fishes in U.S. Reservoirs," Reservoir Fishery Resources Symposium, Athens, Ga., April, 1967, Publ. by So. Div., Amer. Fish. Soc., pp. 298-321.

Jenkins, M. and Morais, I., 1971, "Reservoir Sport Fishing Effort and Harvest in Relation to Environmental Variables," p. 371-384, In G. E. Hall (ed.), Reservoir Fisheries and Limnology, Amer. Fish. Soc., Spec. Publ. No. 8.

Keith, W. E., 1975, "Management by Water Level Minipulation," in Black Bass Biology and Management, Sport Fishing Institute, Washington, D. C.

Klopatek, J. and Risser, P. G., 1977, "Productivity Profile of Oklahoma," Technical Report No. 3, Oklahoma Biological Survey, Norman, Ok.

Leopold, L. B., 1969, "Quantitative Comparison of Some Aesthetic Factors Among Rivers," Geological Survey Circular 620 Washington, D.C.

Lindsey, A. A., Schmelz, D. V. and Nichols, S. A., 1969, "Natural Areas in Indiana and Their Preservation," Indiana Natural Areas Survey, Fafayette, Indiana.

Lower Mississippi Valley Division, 1976, "A Tentative Habitat Evaluation System (HES) for Water Resources Planning," CE, Visksburg, Mississippi.

Markofsky, M. and Harleman, D. R., 1971, "A Predictive Model for Thermal Stratification and Water Quality in Reservoirs," Publ. 16130 DJH 01/71, Environmental Protection Agency, Washington, D.C.

McGimsey, C. R. III, 1973, "Archeology and Archeological Resources," Society for American Archeology, Washington, D.C.

Nemerow, N. L., 1974, Scientific Stream Pollution Analysis, McGraw-Hill Book Company, New York, N.Y.

Odum, P., 1971, Fundamentals of Ecology, W. B. Saunders Co., Philapelphia, Pa.

Ortolano, L., ed., 1973, "Analyzing the Environmental Impacts of Water Projects," U.S. Army Engineer Institute for Water Resources, Ft. Belvoir, Virginia.

Patten, B. C., 1962, "Species Diversity in Net Phytoplankton of Raritan Bay," Jour. Mar. Res., 20: 57-75.

Patten, B. C., et al., 1975, Total Ecosystem Model for a Cove in Lake Texoma, System Analysis and Simulation in Ecology, Vol. 3, Academic Press, New York.

Peet, R. K., 1974, "The Measurement of Species Diversity," Ann. Rev. Ecological Systems, 5: 285-308

Pierce, P. C., Frey, F. E. and Yawn, H. M., 1963, An Evaluation of Fishery Management Techniques Utilizing Winter Drawdowns. Proc. 17th Annual Conf. Southeast Assoc. Game and Fish Comm. 17: 347-363.

Poole, R. W., 1974, "An Introduction to Quantitative Ecology," McGraw-Hill Co., New York.

Ransom, D. and Dorris, C., 1972, "Analyses of Benthic Community Structure in a Reservoir by Use of Diversity Indices," Amer. Midl. Natur., 87: 434-447.

Ricker, W. E., ed., 1968, "Methods for Assessment of Fish Production in Fresh Waters," IBP Handbook No. 3, Blackwell Scientific Publ., Oxford and Edinburgh.

Risser, P. G., 1975, "Identification and Evaluation of Significant Environmental Impacts on Terrestraal Ecosystems," in the Biological Significance of Environmental Impacts, Nuclear Reg. Comm. NR-Conf.-002, Washington, D.C.

Sawyer, C. N. and McCarty, P. L., 1967. Chemistry for Sanitary Engineers, Second Edition, McGraw-Hill Book Company, New York, N.Y.

Schwartz, W. and Schwartz, R., 1959, "The Wild Mammals of Missouri," Univ. of Mo. Press, Columbia, Missouri.

Singh, J. S., Lauenroth, W. K. and Steinhurst, R. K., 1975, "Review and Assessment of Various Techniques for Estimating New Aerial Primary Production of Grassland Harvest Data," Bot. Rev. 41: 181-232.

Soil Conservation Service, U.S. Department of Agriculture, 1974, "Enrivonmental Assessment Procedure," Washington, D.C.

Solomon, R. C., et al., 1977, "Water Resources Assessment Methodology (WRAM) - Impact Assessment and Alternative Evaluation," Technical Report Y-77-1, Wes, Vicksburg, Miss.

"Standard Methods for Examination of Water and Wastewater," 1976, 14th. edition, American Public Health Association, Washington, D.C.

Stoddard, L. A. and Smith, A. D., 1955, Range Management, McGraw-Hill Co., New York.

Teal, J. and Kanwisher, J., 1970, "Total Energy Balance in Salt Marsh Grasses," Ecology 51: 690-695.

Thomas, J. W., et al., 1976, "Guidelines for Maintaining and Enhancing Wildlife Habitat in Forest Management in Blue Mountains of Oregon and Washington," Trans. 41st North American Wildlife and National Resources Conference, Washington, D.C.

Thomas, W. A., ed., 1972, Indicators of Environmental Quality, Environmental Science Research Series, Vol. 1, Plenum Press, New York, 1972.

Tulsa District, U.S. Army Corps of Engineers, 1972, "Matrix Analysis of Alternatives for Water Resources Development," Draft Technical Paper, Tulsa, Ok.

Turner, D. B., 1969, "Workbook of Atmospheric Dispersion Estimates," rev. ed., Publ. AP-26, Environmental Protection Agency, Research Triangle Park, N.C.

U.S. Department of the Army, 1975, "Handbook for Environmental Impact Analysis," Publication No. 200-1, Washington, D.C.

Urban Institute, Inc., 1976, "Land Development and the Natural Environment," report prepared for Department f Housing and Urban Development, Washington, D.C.

Velz, C. J., 1970, Applied Stream Sanitation, Wiley-Inter-Science Book Company, New York.

Voorhees and Associates, Inc., 1975, "In erim Guide for Environmental Assessment," report submitted to Department of Housing and Urban Development, Washington, D.C.

Wharton, C. H., 1970, "The Southern River Swamp-A Multiple-Use Environment," Bureau of Business and Economic Research, School of Business Administration, Georgia State University, Atlanta, Ga.

Wetzel, E. R., 1975, Limnology, W. B. Saunders Co., Philadelphia, Pa.

Wilhm, L., 1970, "Range of Diversity Index in Benthic Macro-invertebrate Populations, Jour. Water Poll. Control Fed., 42, R 221-R 224.

Wistendahl, W. A. and Lewis, K. P., 1972, "Willow Island Locks and Dam," Corps of Engineers, Huntington, West Virginia.

Yeager, L. E., 1949, "Effect of Permanent Flooding in a River-bottom Timber Area," Ill. Natur. Hist. Surv., 25: 33-65.

Salinity, 7, 12, 123, 124
Sediment yield, 50
Smog, 152, 154
Soil chemistry, 5, 12, 51, 52
Soil erosion, 4, 12, 49, 50, 51
Sound, 10, 12, 181
Sound pressure level, 164, 166
Species diversity, 5, 8, 12, 55, 56, 63, 144, 145
Sport fish, 5, 12, 67
State and Local Historical Commissions/Societies, 184
State Department of Wildlife Conservation, 78
State Historical Preservation Officers, 184
Stream habitat, 6, 12, 13, 27, 79, 85
Stream assimilative capacity, 8, 12, 134, 135
Stream flow variations, 8, 12, 136, 138
Suspended solids, 7, 12, 105, 106, 107

Thermal Stratification, 111
Threatened or endangered species, 173
Total dissolved solids, 7, 12, 116, 117
Toxic substances, 7, 12, 127, 128
Turbidity, 7, 12, 104, 105, 106, 107
U.S. Public Health Service Drinking Water Standards, 125, 126, 132
Upland forest habitat, 4, 12, 13, 27, 35
Upland game birds, 3, 12, 24

Variety within vegetation type, 9, 12, 169

Water temperature, 7, 12, 109, 110
Waterfowl, 6, 12, 76
Wetlands, 58, 78
Wetland vegetation, 5, 12, 61
Width and alignment, 9, 112, 167

Zoologist, 172, 173, 174
Zooplankton, 5, 12, 63, 64, 65